a little more

Margaret Scott

a little more

Celebrating a life of letters

Summerhill Publishing

Summerhill Publishing Pty Ltd
92 Warwick Street
Hobart 7000
Tasmania

publisher@summerhillpublishing.com
www.summerhillpublishing.com

The project was assisted through
Arts Tasmania by the Minister for the Arts.

Tasmania

ARTS TASMANIA

Margaret Scott: a little more
Celebrating a life of letters
ISBN 0-9757460-0-6

Design and typesetting: Summerhill Publishing
Cover design: Justy Phillips
Cover photography: Alan Moyle
Inside front cover print: Barbie Kjar
Inside back cover collage: Paul Boam
Printed in Tasmania by Penfold Buscombe

Tribute to a Tasmanian Tiger

From old England in a lather of energies and cardigans,
Over half a dozen seas, across burning countries
Reeking of incomprehensible cooking, migrants came.

Many were eager, but few so thoroughly
Alive and invested with abundant talents, none so
Rich with budding literary potential as this restless
Girl landed on Van Diemen's Land (which seemed
Almost familiar, yet fields were 'paddocks', trees inflammable)—
Rara avis, one of us! chortled the bright parrots—
Excelsior! she said, and made herself at home, at once
Turning to the matter of having a number of children.

Sensible person! as well as witty, deeply schooled,
Creative to within an inch of her life, and also
Overly generous to her many friends—so let me offer a
Toast to a long and happy future: a panegyric
To a remarkable person, in the garb of an acrostic encomium.

John Tranter

Acknowledgements

We would like to acknowledge the many periodicals, books and anthologies in which the works of Margaret Scott have appeared, and to thank the publishers for their kind permission to reproduce some of those works. Given such generosity we trust we have not overlooked anyone in this regard.

Thanks, too, to Stephen Edgar, who worked with Margaret Scott to make this rich and varied selection, and to those of her many friends and colleagues who wrote such unstinted and affectionate tributes to the grande dame of Australian literature. Their names appear under the pieces they wrote throughout the book.

We would like to also thank Arts Tasmania for their support, and especially Lynne Uptin and Gail Cork, who generously shared their experience and knowledge.

Finally, thanks to Patsy Hollis and Fred Baker for checking, editing, gently bickering about hyphens or lack thereof, and generally having a good time working with such wonderful words.

Because of time restraints, not everyone who wished to contribute could meet the rather short deadlines we had for the project, so we have set up a special web site to enable more tributes to be published online. You'll find it here:

www.leatherwoodonline.com/scott

Allan Moult
Summerhill Publishing

Contents

Selected Prose by Margaret Scott

Selected Essays by Margaret Scott

Margaret Scott, by her friends

Foreword

Margaret Scott has an extraordinary range of skills—poet, novelist, short story writer, script writer, essayist, critic, historian, editor, lecturer, broadcaster, social scientist, debater, television panellist, literary judge, and has achieved much in every field.

Born in Bristol, she read English at Cambridge, and after working in a false eyelash factory (a detail that I find irresistible), then as a teacher, she migrated to Tasmania in 1959. She planned to stay there for only two years, but soon succumbed to its powerful appeal and became a permanent resident.

She lectured in the English Department of the University of Tasmania for twenty four years. She wrote her PhD on 'the murderous Machiavel'.

In 1997 she published *Port Arthur: A Story of Strength and Courage*, the best and most moving account of the massacre of 1996 and its significance. In 2000 *Family Album: A Novel of Secrets and Memories* was published—richly layered, poetically written, psychologically penetrating, full of social history and deep insights.

I first met Margaret when we sat on a judging panel for the Victorian Premier's Literary Awards in 1992. I had read two volumes of her poems, *Tricks of Memory* (1980) and *Visitors* (1983) and her novel *The Baby Farmer* (1990), later re-named as *In the Shadows*, a horrifying account of a murder in the 1870s.

I also appeared with her several times on the ABC Television program *Good News Week*, and enjoyed her acid wit.

In 2000 I became Chair of the Port Arthur Historic Site Management Authority (PAHSMA) in 2000 and on my nomination the Tasmanian Government appointed Margaret to the Board in October of that year. In this role she has been of great service to the site and the State, despite her periods of serious illness and the loss in a fire of her home and library.

She was instrumental in establishing the Tasman Institute of Conservation and Convict Studies (TICCS) and inspired the Islands of Vanishment Conference, co-sponsored with Australia ICOMOS, and held at Port Arthur in June 2002. It was hailed as a triumph.

When I was still writing my autobiography, *A Thinking Reed* for Allen & Unwin, Margaret offered advice, both critical and sensitive, on drafts that I gave her. I have great faith in her literary judgment. I love and admire her. She has shown great courage and resilience in overcoming the blows life has dealt her.

She is a poet of compelling insight, and her prose is poetic as well. Her novels, short stories and essays are all of high distinction.

Margaret richly deserved the Emeritus Award of the Australia Council's Literature Board.

Barry Jones
AO, FAA, FAHA, FTSE, FASSA
Former Chair of the Port Arthur Historic Site Management Authority

Introduction

When Margaret asked me to accept this award for her I asked if she'd like to write down what she wanted me to say. She said, 'No, no, no, no. That wouldn't do at all!' So I said 'Well, what would you say if you were there?' And she said, 'I'd say 'Thankyou very much for this award', or words to that effect.'

Well it's 'the words to that effect' that make all the difference. In fact they could perhaps be said to distinguish the writer's use of words—to evoke an experience—from the daily use of words to transmit a content.

Obviously I am not capable of using words 'to that effect' as Margaret would have done. But I am able to do something which she has repeatedly proved herself quite incapable of doing, and that is to say how outstanding she is both as a writer and as a person. She is, I think, a person to whom words like 'amazing' and 'awesome', which spring so readily and loosely to people's lips nowadays, can quite strictly be applied.

Margaret was born in Bristol in 1934. She read English at Cambridge after winning scholarships to both Oxford and Cambridge, at a time when it was still far from usual for women to have tertiary education She was part of a bohemian literary group which included Ted Hughes and Sylvia Plath. After graduating, and marrying, she taught in schools and worked in a false eyelash factory before coming to Hobart in 1959 with her husband and baby son. In the next years she had another son and a daughter and in 1964 was divorced. In 1966 she joined the English Department of the University of Tasmania, of which James McAuley, who became a close friend, was professor. While teaching in the University she completed a PhD.

She had moved to Fern Tree, halfway up Mt Wellington. In the devastating bushfires which swept through Tasmania in 1967 the house was burnt to the ground and she escaped with her children, the dog and the clothes she was wearing. Everything else, including manuscripts of all she had written—a number of unfinished novels and many poems—was destroyed.

Margaret is undoubtedly the most resilient and dauntless person I have ever known. Without any Pollyanna-ish making the best of things she seemed to experience this loss of all she had accumulated as a liberation into a new life. Her poems began to appear in literary journals and in time she published two slim volumes—*Tricks of Memory* in 1980 and *Visited* in 1983.

She and a legal scholar, Michael Scott, had fallen in love and in 1969 they moved into a beautiful old house in Hobart with a composite group of children from their previous marriages and, after 1972, their daughter Sarah. Their house became a place around which writers and artists and people who thought about things eddied. Margaret is extraordinarily welcoming, interesting and interested, riotously funny and a superb cook. She has strong convictions without being judgemental and seems to have time for everybody.

Michael Scott died in 1984 and Margaret decided to leave Hobart. She found a derelict house called Tara on the Tasman Peninsula and spent four years painstakingly restoring it to a state that I think surpassed its former glory. She herself

Acceptance speech on Margaret's behalf for the Alice Award, presented by the Society of Women Writers (Sydney 2000)

stripped all the woodwork. With a fine brush she coloured in the tiny flowers and tendrils in the pressed metal lining the long hall. She created a garden that spilled over with fragrance and colour and a traditional herb garden in the shape of a wheel.

In 1985 she and the poet Vivian Smith together edited an anthology, *Effects of Light: The Poetry of Tasmania.* In 1988 her third volume of poetry, *The Black Swans,* appeared. In 1989 she retired from the University of Tasmania to become a full-time writer. And in 1990 she published her first novel, *The Baby Farmer,* republished in 2002 as *In the Shadows.*

The new house not only drew Hobart friends and visiting writers and scholars but became one of the focus points of local life on the Tasman peninsula. Margaret embraced this area not only for its unique beauty, which she has evoked in many poems, but also for the rare qualities she found in the community—the warmth, matter-of-fact kindness and generosity and undistorted humanity. She has seen in Tasmania a microcosm of all that is Australian, and in the Tasman peninsula she found a microcosm of Tasmania, another rendering down to an essence.

This experience underlies her book *Port Arthur: A Story of Strength and Courage,* 1997, about the Port Arthur massacre of April 1996 when gunman Martin Bryant killed thirty-five people, including children, and wounded many others. She brings her impressive scholarliness to the organisation of the immense jumble of evidence, verbal testimony, police, government and legal records without diminishing the warmth and compassion with which she records the events. The real focus of the book is on the quiet heroism and undramatic strength of the whole community, the anonymous menders of the fabric of local life.

In the next years Margaret began to emerge as a public figure. She was invited to make regular appearances on the TV show *Good News Week* and in the *Great Debate* series. She took part in a TV documentary on the Tall Ships which involved being flown about in a helicopter wearing an orange boiler suit and cone-shaped helmet. Her TV appearances in turn led to a wide range of public-speaking engagements all over Australia—keynote speaker at the conference of nurses in Adelaide, addresses to the Meeting of the Generations conference in Sydney, the Potato Growers Association of Tasmania and the Australian Association of Undertakers (who presented her with a lead and bronze plaque). In 1999 she was awarded an Honorary Doctorate of Letters by the University of Tasmania.

Undistracted by the trappings of fame Margaret continued to write and in 2000 published three major books—*Collected Poems, Changing Countries* and *Family Album.* About a year later an electrical fire broke out while Margaret was absent— and the house she had in effect created, together with all her manuscripts, paintings, books and possessions of every kind burnt to the ground.

It seems unbelievable that anyone could rise renewed from this second lot of ashes but that is what Margaret has done, perhaps not so much like a phoenix as like those Australian trees which need fire to renew themselves. She felt, of course, a profound sense of loss, but also some flicker of exhilaration at the thought of a new start, the lack of encumbrance. She was immediately lent a house in the neighbourhood and has lived there since the fire, planning her new house to be built on the site of Tara. Typically it is to be nothing like the old Tara but designed specifically for present lifestyle and needs. Meanwhile she continues to write and to be involved in local affairs. She is on the board of the Port Arthur Historical Site Management Authority which meets under the chairmanship of Barry Jones. She is passionate about achieving world's best practice standards in conservation, also for other at present neglected convict sites.

Her first novel *The Baby Farmer* had already shown the mastery of Margaret's prose, her ear for speech inflections and her quite unusual ability to present huge dynamic crowd scenes—the handling of mass and detail with the ease of a Delacroix. Her second novel, *Family Album,* is an intricately layered and richly inlaid double narrative of two families, one contemporary and the other Victorian. It belongs with A S Byatt's *Possession* rather than with any contemporary Australian novel. It takes elements of the Victorian novel—the reversal of fortunes, the cruel step-parent, the complications of relationships—but goes beyond pastiche in placing these elements in a framework of psychological realism rather than the Victorian moral framework.

Changing Countries is a collection of stories and essays interspersed with poems. Margaret writes in her foreword that just as the 'I' of the pieces changes countries 'so many other characters quit the territory of memory to begin new lives in fiction' (which is, I think, a very good way of expressing the relation between fact and fiction). The pieces show an unselfrighteous eye for the hypocrisy, greed and callousness underlying many human relationships. There are some delightful stories about childhood, brilliantly told from the child's point of view with its unverifiable but unshakable conviction.

Margaret Scott's *Collected Poems* covers a wide range, from earlier rhymed and regular stanzaed pieces to later freer meditative speech rhythms, from recollections of childhood in Bristol to poems on the beauty of the Tasmanian landscape. They are full of sharply particular detail and breadth of cultural reference. What for me makes them outstanding, and also makes them so accessible, is that whatever she is writing about—jam making or the shape of a rocky island—she is writing about aspects of the self and its ways of experiencing its life. Where the prose works create a fictional but credible context for experience, the poems speak directly out of the experience, seeking to make it recognisable on its own terms. Reality gets its meaning from individual experience, it becomes metaphorical and the poem can move without boundaries from an outer to an inner reality:

> *The house creaked on Sunday afternoons, slept in its weight like an old horse in the sun while across the unmown fields of still brown grass a longing to make something happen rushed like a wind into a vacuum.*

We must be grateful that this body of work escaped from the flames to the safety of print. They show Margaret at the height of her achievement, in prose and in verse, an achievement now recognised by this award.

Sybil Smith
Writer

a little more

Selected Poetry

Stories of my mother's childhood, told in wartime

From the album of my mother's mind,
secret in their innocence,
the dead walked out in comic hats
to posture in a new pretence.

My uncles, always young and smart,
in Norfolk jackets cut the hay,
and Granny in a long white frock
tripped abroad to gather may.

Embowered in abundant peace,
the farm where all the Farrs were born
rose tranquilly amid its flocks,
its blossom trees and golden corn.

The winters of the war were cold.
The people hid in smelly lairs.
But we hid out in Gloucestershire,
in a cupboard underneath the stairs.

I knew we'd have it all one day,
just as Grandpa meant we should.
We'd feed the hens, and milk the cows
and go for picnics in the wood.

I didn't know that Grandpa drank
till his cattle and crops had rotted black,
and the boys went off to die in France
and the burden broke old Granny's back.

And yet my mother never lied
and gave me more than half a fact.
She shared with me the charity
that keeps a dignity intact.

Tricks of Memory (1980)

Surfers

Far out, down heaving green glass hills
the surfers ride the summer seas.
Their taut brown bodies, arms upraised,
slide through an Egyptian frieze.

High and dry upon the beach,
pinned to my rug by a glaring sun
I sit among the picnic things,
alone and fat and forty-one.

And idly through the memory's hand
stream visions of a Cornish day
when effervescent waves and air
sparkled into glinting play.

The breakers crash, a board flies up.
A boy runs laughing on the land,
then, turning, wades to ride again.
I close the fingers of my hand.

Tricks of Memory (1980)

Visiting the maternity hospital

Now I am one of the visitors;
middle-aged, an intruder in outdoor clothes,
watching the tiny, yowling babies through the glass,
mouthing outside the camaraderie
echoes of a cold and grimy chaos,
hidden behind these shining double windows.

The nurses have changed,
but I remember this ward,
where two-day bouts with pain,
Caesareans, breech presentations, stitches
were calmly knitted into a tidy pattern
between our morning tea and the early feed.

Each left and returned on a trolley
to find, alone, a body that obeyed
old, deep-lying forces which broke
the law and order of the will
in earthquake shocks
and threw up life in a tidal wave of muck
to cast the long-nursed dream
on the heart's beach.
Then the unforgettable, unforgotten
was briskly tucked into place
behind the jokes and writing of letters,
and setting of hair.

At three o'clock the visitors came,
mothers of unimagined teenage sons,
borne on a tide of clamorous worry and need
which spent itself about our solid peace,
and died, with claims of past and future time,
under our sweet absorption in the now.

Tricks of Memory (1980)

The house where I was born

The house where I was born
was high, insubstantial and dark,
skeletal with early fears of shadowed rooms,
huge and vague,
crumbling noiselessly
under the soft, massive flow of night tides.

The silly little candle joggled on.
What shrieked once
when the monstrous waves,
poised on the walls,
swept down and swallowed it whole
in their python jaws?

Tonight my parents have the album out.
Sunny children beam from the well-lit page.
The mother speaks of poky rooms she kept
and touches paper hands across the years.
Outside the darkness coils against the glass
and mouths and mouths its meal of long-lost bones.

Visited (1983)

A legacy

His mother's garden throve with vines of beans,
leafy ladderways up the dreaming blue,
and ropes to swing and ring the giant's sun.
Pumpkins for coaches swelled in the fig tree's shade
where fruit as plump as ancient copper jars
dripped juice like oil and honey on the earth.
Hesperides of golden apples shone,
lamps in a gentle night of praising leaves.
And sweeter than the breath of quiet thyme,
those sacred herbs of innocence and grace
fed all the air with rich, sustaining scent.
Then sheaves of green and stores of ripened fruit
were harvested to make a festival,
a table spread where stooks of corn rejoiced.
And the spirit, blessed in love and lore, soared out
to whet its silver wings for distant flight
and sing undaunted up the winter sky.

Visited (1983)

Meeting

I remember when the building
where you worked
stood tense with self-control,
keeping its windows still
as demure eyelids,
gripping itself in joy
around the certainty
that it was different
from any other office block
in the world.

At five o'clock
the sudden flood of clerks,
making a show of crowding
down the steps
like anyone intent
on getting home,
knew themselves, I was sure,
as a chosen people
because you walked
among them,
coming to catch my hand.

Leaving home

'There's happenings I have here,'
said the old woman, touching her webby hair.
'One's a morning early, waking at dawn
in a crowded, crouching cottage dank as toadstools,
taking my best things damp from the dark drawer,
creaking downstairs, trying to eat at a heavy wooden table
moored to stone flags in the flood of day coming,
my box all corded heaved on my father's shoulder
and out in the lush, thick-scented garden
shivering sunshine.
Hollyhocks up to the eaves breasting the mist,
docks like great wet tongues lapping the pump,
soaking grass doused with sparkles round by the privy,
roses tangled in woodbine, flopping with dew
doubling down to the snailed-silver pansies,
nettles with leaves like spades by the pig-pen wall,
lilacs showered in blaze by the open gate.
Out on the road there's the hedge spilling
scrambling nightshirts and starling gabble—
'Goodbye, sissy, don't forget to send!'
If it hadn't been for the chill in my stomach
and the pinch of my good shoes I'd have flown the midden
and swung aloft over the bursting orchard.
Where was I going? Into service or off to my mother's sister
who needed a hand. Maybe a well-off someone
with a house by the sea and a fortune
had taken a fancy. No such thing you say?
But when you're old dreams grow over your days
like weeds in rubble,
all of them morning-wild and free for picking,
all of them love's true heady-scented tokens.'

Visited (1983)

Notice to quit

Rust's blighted my roof.
The dormers gape in quaint deadpan dismay
from a heaving slough of brown corroded tin.
'Look!' cries the man from the council
crashing his boot down on my parlour floor.

'Your foundations've gone, lady.'
A knick-knack shatters in an upstairs room.
My lost love, clear-eyed, stern and trim
in high-romantic khaki,
leaps for the maidenhair.
A mantelpiece of stars of vaudeville
clatters like showgirls' heels
to a long, jangling groan from the piano.

When the dust settles, the sun's a subtler spy.
He probes my ochre frills
and lies in wait in the nook on the back verandah.
He shrinks the withered boards,
points up derisively the crazy swoop
of my ragged iron lace,
clinging by rotten teeth among the vines.

'They wouldn't turn you out at your age, dear!'
Old Amy Vavasour—
the stage-door johnnies called her Twinkletoes—
weeps in the wicker chair
among my ferns and cats.
Implacable light touches a runnel of kohl
on her pastry cheek.

But my tabby has the way of it.
Poor old boulevardier,
long past all that epic dash and swagger,
played out in the rooftop moon's machine-gun nests,
he wears his baggy trousers with an air.

Visited (1983)

Down but not out, like Charlie in *The Tramp*
he mooches from his lair in the peonies.
The timing of that sudden hop and skip
slap-bang on the prosing sun
could bring the house down.

The witch (1)

I was sorting herbs when I heard the window
thump and shatter like an icy wave breaking,
drenching me through with terror of crystal nights.
But there was no torrent of townsfolk,
foaming with torches, roaring to find
the devil's mark on my body—
no one but two little mousy, whey-faced children,
left to die in the forest and weak with hunger.

It seemed a spell had been broken—
the thorn hedge down, the kiss bestowed,
the cottage filled with life again and laughter.
Baking bread with little Gretel,
smoothing Hansel's pillow, the old frog
became, I thought, as fair and virtuous
as any youngest daughter of a king.
But they were living out another story.

I sit by the fire in the smell of my burned flesh,
held very still over the pain.
My eye goes down the fender
to the riddle of the smashed clock and the broken chair.
My owl trails his wing.
I am in hiding from what has happened here.
Soon I'll be picking the charred cloth from the burns,
touching and touching again
to see what can be borne.
Then the memory's witch-hunt will break up
the boards of my skull and drag me,
changed to a red-eyed devil's hag,
through streets of unrecognised days,
past murderous innocent eyes
to the inconceivable thrusting into the flame.

Visited (1983)

Walking to the hospital

The city's so quiet on this mild autumn Sunday
you can hear someone
clearing out bottles in a backyard.
The trumpet from an upstairs record-player
rises in blue-red jets through the tranquil air.
I am walking to see a friend in the hospital,
to report I have fed her cat and watered her plants.

In her house the tick of her clock
drips steadily down to spread in pools of light
over the bland even sheen of her parquet floor.
She has cleared her desk of all but
the glint and shade of her walnut tree.
The Siamese clocks in
through his flap in the kitchen door.

There and in this street I move quietly
as though to catch behind indifferent stillness
and the tinny incongruities of grief
some meaning in the wasting of her light,
some ringing answer in my ticking blood.

Visited (1983)

Settlers' graveyard

None of these gaunt stones was raised to an old man,
and most stand over narrow graves like cribs.
One granite pillar, gritting texts like teeth
in the south wind, records the deaths of Karl and Anna Möller,
parents to a long graven register of beloveds.
In this bleak dormitory where only the grass whispers
they laid to rest eleven sons and daughters
knowing them in the sacrament of absence.
A towering, ragged land. Here a mother could run
madder than Lear with a skeletal fool for comfort
mouthing night and clacking along behind her.
But the migrant woman, tying on laundered aprons,
stirred ritual possets, laid on poultices,
closed the eyes and prayed; dressed in her crackling blacks
and trailed the coffins in their long procession
out to this dour hill. Like Pyrrha she swept home
from the harsh field where the stones trembled to life
in her steady vision: the homes, the river, the valley,
the seas she'd crossed, all distant homelands
seared in a fiery shroud of amazing trumpets;
and her children, the chosen, rising elect and whole,
spurning the splitting stone and the shrieking wicked,
coming in joy for their last long Bible story,
and garnered warm and white within her arms.
Almost the apocalyptic murmur of these bones
cries pity for the cold earth, the unrepentant waste.

Visited (1983)

Housework
1 Making redcurrant jelly
for Beverley Farmer

Today I made redcurrant jelly,
lugging a pan of juice as thick and dark as
water dyed by my grandmother's heavy curtains.
And the face I found in my white enamel well,
looking up from a crimson mirror, was hers to the life
when she bent to knead a trough of steaming rep.
There were her plump cheeks split by shadows,
a glint of spectacles, her horns and wisps of hair.
When I was young she used to tell us stories
of mirrors that spoke in riddles, miraculous wells,
innocent victims of magic, great survivors,
but her eyes that are also mine discouraged questions.
What made the daughter run with her jar to the spring
or the mother carry soup for a stranger god?
As I stirred in sugar the sealed face dissolved
in a swirl of baffling mothers, importunate girls,
labouring since the time that pots were fired
to draw reflecting water from the earth,
to scour, steep, launder, rinse, refine,
to mix soup, remedies, ale, lye, preserves,
recreating always the same image:
vessels of dark fluid, women tied by blood,
brewing, pouring knowledge that goes beyond them.

The Black Swans (1988)

2 Polishing the step

The front step's covered with a thin brass skin
that I polish up once in a blue moon,
washing it first, then wiping on clots
of Brasso that curdle to poisonous green
and rub off black until, if I keep at it,
a rippling jaundiced face with hangdog eyes
looks up from a sheet of glint. But it won't last.
Settling fogs, salt-laden evening damps
will breathe it dull again in a week or two.
Earlier women had daily trysts with this step.

After cleaning the range and scrubbing the
whitewood table they'd kneel to meet
lugubrious reflections, queerer still
than those the world gave back—brazen hussy,
golden-hearted treasure. All lost, all gone.
The metal never admits to an old lie.
It's little wonder brass has a bad name,
impervious, blatant, lacking in charity,
or that poets, seeing their elbow grease go
for nothing, their images fade,
write verses damning brass and sluttish time
and pin their faith on polishing a rhyme.

4 Mending a dress

I am sitting mending the sleeve of an old dress.
Light from a big yellow lamp falls on a fold
of blue cotton like evening sun, stroking the downy nap
until it smiles. A car hums in the street.
A log stirs in the fire. The dress lies warm in my lap
like a friendly cat. I am not thinking much
about the past when kingfisher blue flashed
at the tail of my eye, dipping through shadow and gleam
in a forest of windows. I'm not thinking much
about the future when one day, old and bent,
I'll find the dress pushed to the bottom of a ragbag,
its blue brittle and thin as the wings of moths.
I am just poking the needle in and out
bringing together two segments of frayed cloth
under the arm. As I turn the cotton this way
and that I see that I'm making a seam,
a dark line like a straight creek lying between
blue fields where, traffic lulled to a hum,
a comfortable cat smiles and stirs, warm
as a dozing log, where a kingfisher flies in the trees
and moths come down to dance in the golden light
of the present moment.

The Black Swans (1988)

Hobart Snow
for Andrew Sant

Snow lies thick in this city once in a lifetime.
For years it keeps to the mountains,
breathes in the wind from the south,
troubling the people with myths of the great untamed.
But one night, as we sat by the fire,
eating and drinking in Andrew's house on the hill,
out of the luminous sky,
swirling across the window that looks to sea,
down it came!
We ran and gazed up in a crowd
at air alive with sailing, wiry grey
as though all the ratlines and halyards of a huge ship
were reeling and sliding down to the swallowing earth
in flick after flick of an eye.
Out in the road, perfectly sober men
were whooping away like owls,
laughing and dodging about between parked cars—
Holdens and sullen Toyotas, rugged white,
humping their backs like cattle against the wind.
Down in the little garden the earth was wet,
flakes hissing and dying like matches among the plants,
yet already, as night drew on, a ministering frost
was secretly working the damp to the snow's pitch.
It was hard getting home,
harder to sleep in the knowledge of all that
stealthy, perpetual flying and soft settling.
At dawn it was all there—the virgin roofs,
the streets like country lanes on Christmas cards,
neighbours in dressing-gowns hurrying out with cameras,
and everyone talking together as they never did—
a helmeted youth on his skis,
a child rolling a lumpy ball of snow
round and round on a little trampled lawn—
as though in the night some predator out of the waste
had slipped in among us to lie by a fire and sleep.

The Black Swans (1988)

Glove

At the back of this old drawer there's a lost glove,
crinkled, lifeless, dry as a sloughed skin—
a kid glove with tiny raised seams
that ran between the knuckles in the days
when every lady matched her hats and bags
and cocked her head before she went to town,
judging a gloved hand held at arm's length
like a mirror.
But this is a poor black widow.
Impossible to imagine any lover
gathering it up to cherish as a favour,
yearning over its freedom to touch a cheek,
plotting to carry it back where it makes a pair.
Loss has made it useless and absurd.
This glove can't keep the world at bay
for horsemen or gardeners. It carries infection—
an outcast, black as mobbed crow, dead witch.
Touch it gingerly then,
remembering Borgia gifts breathing perfumed vapour,
Jack Palance and his black killing glove.
The hand's mask. Only the wicked and false
would wear such gloves—stranglers, cracksmen,
fat white ladies whom nobody loves.

Unknown causes

Uncle Reg smelled of Wills' tobacco
and when I asked about Granny or the war
took to groping in pockets for cigarette cards
of British mammals, butterflies and flowers.
We'd sit and sort out cabbage-whites and voles
in the poky lace-curtained bay window
that crouched like a birdwatcher's hide
on the Highbury road. Sleeves brushed
the glass and trams went idling by like big game.
Upstairs my grandmother heaved in her blind bed,
thumping the ceiling and all day squawking for Reg
to come with his medals and Mauser and cut a swathe
through her thickets of black, sibilant fever.

Mother and son dwindled to sepia studies
of a second lieutenant and a Lily Langtry pose,
a nest egg put away in the savings bank,
an album filled with mounted cards in sets.
I opened it first on the floor of our cold kitchen
one evening when supper was late. My mother
humped about in the old blue hat she wore
for scrubbing steps, crying and asking
meaningless, outraged questions until
the beaver I'd never found, the meadowsweet
(Spiraea ulmaria) and the missing
number thirty, the swallowtail, shrank
and gave out a thin treacherous scent.

Later a cousin, lethal with secrets, whispered
how, after Granny's funeral, Uncle Reg
was found in the lake on the common.
I pictured his coat winnowing under his arms
like stingray fins, bearing him gently
among the shrieking ducks as the fish
nibbled his fingers and asked nothing.

The Black Swans (1988)

Evening at the farm

The sun winks from the trees beyond the barn.
Antlered shadows cross the kitchen floor.
As on any other day of unchanged concerns,
the woman, a seemly sack tied in the middle,
stands at the range stirring the supper pots;
the man sits quiet at the heavy table,
his rough hands clasped in a slab of light
on the blond wood. Stream drifts in and out of shadow.
A dead hare, hung on a hook from a beam,
rotates in a cloud of glittering flies.
The blue glaze on its eye, the red drip at its nose
gleam and go dark.
Outside the two boys skitter around the yard
in skinny knickerbockers, flailing their thin arms
like gawky hens. Mother won't speak, won't budge
till the man erupts in a great scraping of boots
and blunders over the flags like a black Cyclops.
His shoulders break like a wave against the sun.
The hare jigs on its pale, grooved haunch, steam billows,
the high playtime voices stop short.
Mother watches her pots, steady as the old black nub
of her survival, while Father sprawls
in short and musty straw in the back barn.
Legs thrown awry, he grips his cider keg,
reeling to the thick oblivion of cattle.

The Black Swans (1988)

After their kind

I am lying flat under an old quilt
moving the memory's eye round lost rooms,
discovering forgotten shapes; texture and shine
rise like the flicker of fish in the murk of the sea.
I name them one by one in the great game
of re-creation: silver candlestick, ebony elephant,
mantelpiece, grandfather clock and hunting print—
the things that crouched to watch the family
gathered at a round table for Sunday dinner.
An interlude:
my father, a British Israelite, is carving beef,
my mother offering advice and serving peas,
my brother, who is doing evolution at school,
mentions the apes. My father drops his knife
and bangs the table: 'God created man
in His own image. D'you think God looks like a monkey?'
Too shocked to giggle I push my potatoes about
making a nice little scenic park in the gravy.
My brother is stubborn for truth, mother near tears.
How could we understand rage in that mild man?
Not even my mother knew how his natural parents,
insolvent, dead or deserting passed him on
to learn to be a stranger couple's son.
Having each other, we had less need to believe
in a stately benevolent Father in nightshirt and beard.
Such readings come like light, the beginning of wisdom,
but how can I conjure that scene in the others' eyes?
Was there a hole in the carpet that bothered my mother,
a smaller elephant, curtains with a meaning different
from the wavy lines of blue I summon up,
a row of clocks muttering away to my father,
another tree, evil or good, in the window,
heavier shadow?
How can I make the descent to another darkness,
that welling ocean-bed of nascent forms,
of objects drowned and changed,
breeding-place of the mind that shapes a world?

The Black Swans (1988)

Shark

At dawn when the black nets billowed and stirred
under the swell of the bay, the great white pointer,
idling up from the south, bloated with seals,
ran foul of the long web. Full grown before Cook was born,
centuries ago he'd drifted quiet as cloud
among the oiled lubras gathering crays.
He might have brushed Bligh's keel off Bruny Island
or shadowed Bass and Flinders on their voyage.
When they hauled him in, a surfie borrowed a ute
and fairly flew up the road to the nearest phone.
The meatworks said they'd send a freezer truck.
Before he got back to the quay he was making millions,
exhibiting city by city across the mainland
the biggest, oldest shark in world history.
But someone with other ideas had taken a chainsaw
and cut off the head. Two fishermen, shoulder to shoulder,
paddling in blood, smiled out through the gaping jaws
in a frame of teeth. The photograph made
the front page in most of the dailies. It's still
in the bar of the pub where visitors stand
looking south to a fading expanse
of buttermilk ocean, blue as a blind eye.
Beyond the mist that veils the distant pole
the waters are hid as with stone and
the face of the deep is frozen. A sail,
a blown white leaf, hangs in the blue like an emblem
and the hills lie all around, chin upon hand.

The Black Swans
for Ruth Blair

The children have taken the boat round the point today.
I sit on the sand with the new binoculars
trying to match the coast of this island bay
with my exile's map. Close by, a white-faced heron
waits for fish. Each hunched in a separate need
we watch the three black swans come out to feed.
The black swans! In Jonson's day the wits
made comic mirrors called 'Antipodes',
mocking the times with virtuous whores, white crows,
ascetic drunks, and black swans, nesting in walking trees.
Even now these birds surprise. Emblems of
paradox, they ride in their dipping line on the blue sea,
sombre as slow, archaic, high-prowed
funeral ships, with the plain absurdity
of cut-out toys, a scrap of nursery frieze.
But when I turn the glasses on a wing, a tough
red beak, a savage scarlet eye, they're suddenly rough
and real, and all themselves.
Their feathers are dull with salt, tattered by wind
to makeshift heaps of burnt-out odds and ends—
a ruffle of charred paper, a draggled quill,
a stirring of buried lice. A neck bends,
thick as a child's arm, to a pointed, violent head,
red eye intent with the beat of scaly leg,
with the thrust of working webs in the clear wave.
They pass like the last of a tribe too wild to beg,
like run-down pirates, gypsies, renegades
with broken teeth, bandanas, belts of knives.
And so they go each morning of their lives
to where the pickings are—as ape men went
or my father in his suit, as the fishing crane
goes out and the fisherman.
When evening comes they travel back again
and sleep as everyone sleeps—and has slept—who must be fed,
whatever coast he maps, whatever stars
shine through the lappings of myth on his quiet bed.

The Black Swans (1988)

Elegies

M.F.C.S. 1928-1984

1

At ten to twelve by the grandfather clock
in the hall you stopped breathing in your sleep.
I put down the telephone and came back
to the study door—as I'd come for years
with questions, news and jokes—
meaning, I think, to tell you you were dead,
but the light of the lamp beat down
on the arm and seat of your chair
and the darkness filled with glimmering books
reeled and shook with your absence as though
from the long stroke of a black bell.
The cat was mewing, mewing down in the kitchen
and I went as on ordinary nights to open a door
but this was the first meeting with life
from the new world in which no search
could find you, so I watched wary of strangeness
as the pleased arch of its back wound round
my legs, and it strolled, taking breath for granted,
down the path. There was no wind.
Nothing but garden trees rising against
the glow of Saturday night and the pulse of silence.

The Black Swans (1988)

2
Friends who mean to be kind speak of a happy release
and it's true that in the week before you died
you couldn't eat or walk, your mind was going.
You spoke of prisons and woke at night from
tormenting dreams of actions for negligence.
Between sips of Sustagen made at three in the
morning you called for documents, gave contrary
directions concerning capital trials and execution.
On the day of your death, your compassionate
philosopher's face broke in chaotic fragments—
a nose sharp as a fin, a flake of dark moustache,
ulcers, a tooth, a harsh bubbling snore.
But time like your bones collapsed in on itself.
Your waking eyes were blue. You said, 'Dear love,
dear love' as tenderly as on that summer night
in the dunes beyond the yacht club.
Holding your hand, I remembered how you sat
by my bed on the day our child was born and,
to take my mind off the pain, gave a most lucid elegant
disquisition on contingent and necessary statements.
The hearing's over now, the case is lost,
our past locked up beyond the reach of proof.

In the garden

I am digging the garden and thinking about old loves
who turn up sudden and shining like daffodil bulbs
in black crumbly spadefuls of years-ago.
Perhaps it's the scent of roses that's set me off
though the gifts I remember best are not the flowers.
This Tony—dark-eyed, a bit overweight, a fine tenor—
scooped the flesh out of half a pineapple
and filled the shell to the brim with Benedictine—
a loving cup to cure my streaming cold.
He proposed one summer Sunday at Maddingley Hall
under magnolia trees, so kind and fatherly,
so little like the extreme, passionate, spiteful run of the mill,
I stuttered, flushed and very nearly took him.
Pressing the bulbs back into damp earth, restoring
the status quo, I wonder about a life in Manchester,
Mrs Headmaster now, it's very likely,
with Oxford sons and a daughter in pharmacy,
my real children nipped, wasted in darkness.
I'm angry at all that power to give or withhold
held by a silly girl who broke with Nick,
languished after a lanky history student,
and married the one who could turn a compliment:
'My love, when a man's walking along with you,
he doesn't need a flower in his buttonhole.'
So off I go, stumping in muddy boots, for a pot
of fuchsia cuttings. That bit of garden's bare
except in spring. I scoop out holes between
the clustered bulbs. Reflecting that it's always
touch-and-go that anything I plant will grow or bloom,
I feel kinder to that younger self, smiling up out of
the chancy weather in Tony's pressed and faded photograph.

The Black Swans (1988)

Bristol: 1942

The days were tame. The usual faces
stooping over their porridge;
the patient plane trees standing in a row;
the park that had always been at the top of the street.
Songs; reading-books; Miss Hemingsley intent
on teaching us how to make pompoms
from scraps of wool,
inspecting fingernails, turning a page
as she read about Jack taking the cow to market.
At supper time Mr Arnold next-door
walked out in the cooling air
to examine his two-foot plot of vegetables,
leaned on our fence to talk about liquid manure—
each day he lay in wait for the milkman's horse—
while beyond the blackout curtain
in the kitchen our mother bustled round
the skinny chairs, setting out
little cubes of rationed butter and
sawing slices of the British loaf.
The siren, voices, running woke us later,
the blind tread of engines,
the howl and earth-splitting crash of the first bomb.
In the shelter we lay and watched
the shaking ceiling,
huddled at the foot of a beanstalk of black air
growing up between our little hoarding lives
and the huge wild profligacy of strangers.

Renovations (date unknown)

Prince

Nearly fifty years ago my parents took Prince away
on a cold spring night. Snap-frozen, it's all
still here—the car grinding out of the drive,
soft flames in the grate, the hulking wireless set,
two empty chairs and mine watching the fire
as I thought of them shepherding Prince down a white passage
and the vet lifting his needle up to the light.
People were shy of touching in the forties
but Prince lay across my feet and licked my hands.
While he muttered and groaned with the sun on his
snoozing nose, I traced the shallow groove between
his eyes and learned the delicate wisps
feathering his legs. The hair on his back was
chestnut shading to umber, wavy like graining
drawn on a varnished door, so dense that when
I dragged my fingers through it, it stayed in furrows.
He steamed ahead on walks to hunt for rabbits,
came down to meet the school bus every day,
loved Marmite, bread and jam, liquorice and cheese.
That spring he scented a bitch on heat in the village,
snuffled around in the garage where she'd slept,
chewed an old rug and ripped up a leather jacket.
Flustered and shamed, my father wrote a cheque.
Prince, chained in the yard, slipped his collar,
came cockily home with a pair of motorbike goggles.
They couldn't discuss it, unable to find any
ground between sniggering and horror. I barely
understood what was driving Prince, screamed
and stormed when I saw what they meant to do.
I didn't brood for long and ceased to see, as wariness
became a way of life, that the cold set in on that night
beside the fire. But dearer than babies, lovers,
my human dead, absurdly, that little death lives
on and on, and Prince, complete in every hair,
comes back—innocent, cheerful, trusting, taken away.

Renovations (date unknown)

Big game

The Maharajah is making a camp for his big game shoot
in the jungle of Assam. Already a road has been cut
all the way from the border of his state to the maidan
he has selected for his purpose. All along the road,
across the bamboo bridges, past swamps where grass nods
over the elephants' heads, come cartloads of double tents,
each one the size of a London drawing room,
with cotton dhurees for carpets, sofas, bathtubs, armchairs
and dressing-tables, four-poster beds, bales of mosquito netting;
chests of spices for the Maharajah's curries;
a silver dinner service for seventy persons;
cases of Gentlemen's Relish and Havana cigars;
an ice-making machine; crate upon crate of Champagne;
flocks of cutlets and breakfasts of devilled kidneys on the hoof;
sixty elephants; four hundred and forty-eight retainers:
an orchestra with a Viennese conductor;
cooks, waiters, mahouts, armourers, tailors;
apothecaries, bakers, bearers and taxidermists;
gardeners to gather flowers for the great shamyanah
where the guests will dine in tails after sundown;
and scouts who will go at dawn in search of game.
Lord Henry Mumford is coming to bag a tiger.

He dreams at night of the varnished yellow globe
his headmaster used to keep in his study corner.
It sprouts flattened ears; oceans snarl away from a black gulf.
Eyes burn out of Mongolia and Persia.
Hyderabad and Shanghai are terrible fangs.
Siam splits in an open-throated roar
'Wretched boy! Vile, cowardly, yellow-livered wretch!'
The tiger is raking his backside with fiery claws
but when he wakes the roaring is far away in the moonlit jungle.

The scouts come in after breakfast. A tiger has made a kill
and is still, they say, certainly close at hand,
lying up full-fed to sleep through the day's heat.
Lord Henry seizes his four-bore elephant rifle.

O vile, cowardly wretch! His stomach riots against his devilled
    kidneys.
'Sahib,' his bearer murmurs, 'not the rifle. Where is the time
for sighting the charging tiger?' He proffers a shotgun
loaded with lead ball. 'Aim, sahib, at the shoulder.
Stop him dead for you must kill him quick if he is coming.'
(A wounded' tiger will leap at an elephant's head,
ripping the mahout, smashing the frail howdah.)
Now the cream of the elephants are ready,
those who will stand like rocks when a tiger charges,
each with her mahout mounted astride her neck.
The sahibs are settled in howdahs fitted with gunracks.
When the guns are all in position the beat begins —
a long line (the flightier elephants) crashing through grey scrub
with a drumming, yelling host trudging up behind.
Thousands of birds reel from shivering trees.
Lord Henry recalls the din of a clamorous scrum,
flight, the study, blood in dark red tongues on his pale thighs
as he edges, whimpering, out of his stiffening breeches.
One of the elephants trumpets in mid-line. The Maharajah
remarks to a rocketing peacock, 'Ah! He has scented
stripes, I do believe!' And there it is in the sunlight,
lithe, massively muscled, hurtling upon Lord Henry,
orange and black, its head as big as the world.
O vile wretch! He throws up the gun. Fires.
Opens his eyes. The tiger lies as quietly as a rug.
All's jubilation and extended hands. On the dusty earth
a crimson tongue, viscous, filmed, pauses, flows,
laps at his booted foot. He prods the creamy belly
with a bloodied toe, elated, wonderfully purged.
A true catharsis.

That night amid glowing Havanas and glimmering shirt-fronts
he expounds the virtues of shotguns over rifles.
There's talk of tomorrow's sport—a day in the marshes—buffalo,
snipe, the chance of a shot at a rhino.
The maharajah promises plenty of bears in the days to come.
And leopards. A general recalls bagging a brute that fought

like the very devil when he'd put five bullets at least
in its spotted hide. They smile and tap their feet
as the orchestra plays a tune from *The Gondoliers*—
'Take a pair of sparkling eyes.' Lord Henry turns in
and dreams his teeth are shotguns blazing away at rhinos.
He engorges the jungle whole in a black mouth.

The cool dry library air

The betrayed come here to the cool dry library air
to take the cure for lungs raddled with quarrels.
People torn open by terrible half-true charges
lie back and take the nourishment of fact,
sipping the names of geological specimens,
tonics compounded of catalogues of moths.
Victims of onslaughts that sent all reason flying
and left them coated with slime from head to foot
feel on their brows the healing hand of an index,
the clean touch of words denoting invertebrates
or eucalypts found in remote Tasmanian rainforest.
Propped on the inhuman kindness of things,
the unyielding shoulder of neat definitive lists,
they ease into forgetfulness of self,
of treacherous unstable concepts like hate and love.

Flowers
for David Ferry

Springtime

We used to go out in the mornings to the bluebell woods
or take baskets for primroses, picked from the dew-cold grass
under hawthorn hedges. There were violets sometimes,
crisp as the sugar flowers on fancy cakes,
cloyingly scented like silks laid up in a press.
We liked the bounty of it—the sheaves of succulent stems
draped over an arm, the basket so full of
small cream fragrant faces, looking up to be fed,
you could hardly have put a pin between the petals.
Massed in bowls and vases around the house
they stood apart, dying with dignity, and when
the evening sun lit up the rooms, wrote
with their shadows, unheeded and blind, on the walls.

Cordylines
When I moved in first and the house was all surrounded
with waist-high grass and hillocks of builders' rubbish,
the cordylines had the gawky, freakish look
of mad old women with feathers in their hair.
Surviving alone from the wreck of the homestead garden,
they kept up a fractious rattle in high winds
and threw down skeletal bunches of dead blossom.
These lay among the broken four-by-twos, tiles and tins
like dusty bouquets dropped by Miss Havisham.
But after the slashing and hoeing, truckloads of loam,
a ton of chicken manure, there's an opulent pelt
of bright green, new-sown lawn, clipped edges,
a full dress circle of pink pelargoniums, fuchsias
and blue-eyed Susans. And—though untouched—
the cordylines have utterly changed their tune.
Leaning together in their tidy island bed,
leggy, exotic and proud as African models,

Renovations (date unknown)

they expect a page in a great Florilegium,
a rustle of tissue, a perfect, hand-tinted engraving,
even a plaque at their feet, Latin on bronze
with 'Presented to the curator of these gardens ...'

Nasturtiums
The nasturtiums are sprouting in hundreds
across the garden. Each seed puts down
a succulent white root, thrusts up a stalk
with two small neat round leaves, winsome
and vividly-green as those comic-book plants
dotted among a child's party of frogs.
I feel like a cruel old witch when I yank them out,
but left to themselves they swell into monstrous mounds—
turtles with heaving shells of soft green platelets,
simmering mobs of pale-eyed parasols
shaken by a raucous babble, a lurid shrieking
more dreadful for lying low in venomous silence.
Sniggering flowers peek out—orange and mustard,
some yolk-yellow with throats as brown as hyenas
or bad teeth, some paler with bulbous foreheads
and dwarfish scowls. The have blood on their chins
and spiky hair on their lips. What a crop!
What a nest of serpents! What can have rotted down
in this mild garden to feed these hysterical leaves
and malevolent blossoms?

Fig
to Gwen Harwood

You sometimes wrote about gardens, fruit and flowers—
your comely Edwardian garden; pippins and grapes;
speedwell, waxflower, musk on a springtime hill—
and often your eye ran back through leaf and colour
to the shape of a lost friend in a net of shadows.
Here at Impression Bay in a convict garden
a fig tree spreads its hands over snaking limbs,
a maze of leafy hollows. Its fruit thrust up
like hearts drawn on a wall—A. loves E.—
or winking lamps set in a green twilight.
Their juice is crimson, warm, irresistibly sweet.
Forget the apple. This is the fruit Eve plucked
and gave to Adam. Imagine him stoking
its nubile curve with a finger, sniffing, nuzzling,
engorging this luscious sap welled from the earth,
this rush of noonday—until on his hot tongue
he feels the roughness of hundreds of tiny seeds
and sees these figs are shaped like falling tears,
sees loss is the shadow cast by an act of love.
On the tree of the knowledge of good and evil grow
fruit that ripen as summer comes to an end,
instants of sweetness defined by a net of darkness.

Renovations (date unknown)

The moon-bow

Clouds come over the hill at the back of the house.
In the garden there's nothing but squat sticks
dark with wet. At evening a bent moon
looks out of the pine trees like an old woman
who keeps a pair of silver dancing shoes
in a yellowing shoe box.
I think of friends in Oxford, Brisbane, Stanford,
leafing through new books and shouting
from cool verandah to leaf-shadowed kitchen
in the heat of debate.
Out in the night the rain comes on again,
fretting at roots and walls, loosening their grip,
edging them down the slope to the dark sea
as the moon on her knobbled feet goes plodding along
through misty gullies and sodden thickets of cloud
in search of kindling.
And then in the black pit under the hill
she lights the moon-bow—
a ghostly, luminous arc like a dancer's spring.
O queen and huntress! You make my flesh creep
back to wondering life.

Renovations (date unknown)

Nocturne

Waking at two in the morning I see the moon
bleaching my bedroom carpet to a colour I can't name.
But then it's years since I had a word with Diana—
virgin, goddess of childbirth, mistress of menstrual blood
and lovers' meetings.
I've turned into a paradox of my own,
huddling my elderly bones in a foetus curl
under frowsy sheets until the moonlight smells
of unwashed clothes.
No more roving for me to that glimmering beach
where the roof of the yacht club pulsed like
a steel drum as we coupled, slippery and salt,
in the taste of sea.
Yet I know by heart the names of my lovers and children
and—if I get up early—as I make the tea
I'll see the moon fade out in brightening sky
as dawn translates the ocean's nameless gleam
to rose and gold.

Renovations (date unknown)

Cancer patient

She used to win prizes in quizzes
held at the golf club. I remember
us standing together on the club house steps
enjoying a cigarette in the interval
between spelling or sports and a round
on world affairs—polite, at ease, well-dressed,
looking up at the stars as though with a touch
we could halt the turning globe.
One night, not six months later, she arrived
at the doctor's wearing a dressing-gown,
shuffled along the hall past the waiting room door
in cornflower blue brushed nylon with satin trim.
Patients in sweaters and sports coats,
trainers and polished brogues looked down at
their magazines, nervous of seeing her reaching
out for rescue like a swimmer caught in a rip,
of hearing out of that wild remorseless current
questions never admitted at the club.

Castaway

Sometimes a neighbour's look, a postcard, a telephone call
will carry you up the shore of another life
and leave you gaping amazed at sudden jungle
a world away from the dolorous desk,
the spruce backyard, the brick-and-tile in Rosebud.
This glimmering shade's cacophonous with
unfamiliar names of long-dead pets and teachers,
side-streets in distant cities and faithless lovers.
The canopy's alive with flitting shapes unknown
beyond the confines of this island.
Here is the castaway's camp, his palisade,
contrivances he's fashioned year by year,
stores he saved from the wreck of his old ship
before it sank from sight beyond the reef.
Fragments of once-proud sails now patch his roof.
A saw, a pannikin hang by the bed
where every day he wakes alone at dawn
to a view of mountains. Those peaks rise
over the trees in a blue scrawl whose message
you seem to have read from a different angle
on the wall of sky to the west of your own island.

Land

The plane climbs she sees the separate places
in her life—streets and parks, the bush beyond the town,
grid of paddocks, beaches edged with foam—
read out as one, a realm, a land like those
story books and hymns she used to sing
where some poor widow's son might save the king
from monstrous perils and win his daughter's hand;
the Spanish find undreamed-of stores of gold;
or saints immortal dwell in pure delight.
Cars bowl along the country roads like beads,
dams twinkle in the sun like scattered coins,
while all around the hills sit patiently,
their shoulders wrapped in capes of fleecy trees.
And far away—two, three days' march at least—
one peak still white with snow burns unconsumed
as though a traveller here might chart a course
and know where in the end his feet would lead.

The oxygen machine

The oxygen machine stands by the bed
high-shouldered in grey enamel,
with a bland sloping brow of users' instructions:
Fill and attach humidifier if required;
Set flow meter to prescribed level;
Keep matches, lighted cigarettes and all other sources
of ignition out of the room where the product is located ...
In crises it seems impervious as a butler,
but press a switch and it sails into keen humming,
broken now and again by blowsy, mechanical sighs
like a tin seal that's laboured across a beach
and is swimming out to the cool life of the sea.
I move in its wake—once the cannula's little horns
are pushed in place—leaving behind the wavering shriek for air.
As our bodies grow gradually easy and more buoyant,
thoughts slip free of the grip of getting a breath,
skimming away like gulls to a calm horizon
and all the reopening otherness beyond.

White Angelus
To Paul Boam

I came in out of the dark to the warm house
where soup purred on the stove and there—there—there
windows opened through wings, the bones of boats,
abraded wood
on shorelines, exultant skies, engulfing seas—
the world as you must see it, looking back
imbued with all your living, peopled by you
the 'I' within the poem.
You have opened, delivered up the places where you walked
stooping to gather feathers and button-grass,
a sheaf of delicate bones, the core of something
long dissolved in water.
You have painted your own face—a bronze Neptune
with sea-salt white in your beard
and the counterpart, the little tumbled figure
more frail than the curled shell of 'The Sea Exults'.
Tracing your path I think I know the name
of the long skeletal head and the savage beak
that tears the gentle wren.
I know the cry of the struggler in the water
and the ageless beat of the waves that ride him down.
Yet names and cries are not what you have fashioned.
Your grammar of paint, your wire and paper rhythms
show how the colours of bone and splintered timber
wind in the rope that reaches the drowning man,
how the wren's blue sleets on the hungry ocean
and glows in the sky where the great sea-eagle soars.
You have not said that something strikes a balance
but have lived it, crafting the fragments of your days
to a marriage of shapes and colors, textures, tones.
All these, defining light by the presence of darkness,
unite in a gift, a welcome, a resolution.

IO

What did she feel as her shoulders thickened,
her arms dropped to the earth and her fingers fused
into black hooves? What sound came as nose and mouth
rushed out in a bony tunnel and horns sprang
from her head? How, in that half second when
her lithe maiden's body swam in the heifer's bulk,
did she see the incredulous faces and the grass
at her feet?
And what did the witnesses make of this flickering image
Zeus, her lover; Hera, the jealous wife;
Argus, the hundred-eyed, who would be her gaoler;
the gadfly, up Hera's sleeve to torment the rival?
Victim, whore, prisoner, nomad, princess,
mother, moon-goddess, paramour, mad cow—
you can't avoid her tragicomic gaze.
Her bewilderment is part of the whole vision
when all the possibilities are present,
like a shoal of fish held in a net of colours—
fish that are also myriads of watching eyes.
Look! They are there when the diver lifts her arms,
when the black lizard touches a lover's shoulder.
And though this woman seated by a vase and flowers
seems quite at home in a normal human shape,
she, too, is poised in a moment of becoming
which opens under the gaze of a school of eyes.

Barbie Kjar monograph (1996)

Margaret Scott, right, at work in her studio at Tara (shown above before and after restoration). Below: At book launches with writer Richard Flanagan, left, and artist Paul Boam.

Opposite, clockwise from top left: Margaret at eighteen months; with brother, David Russell; with David and her parents at The Elms, Severn Valley (1936); son Daniel's wedding at Tara; from left, daughter Kate, Marcus, Margaret, and Daniel; Margaret's graduation from Cambridge (1956).

a little more

Selected Prose

'And thou in this shall find thy monument'

M ost conferences I have attended have brought together members of a single profession: actuaries, potato-growers, undertakers. The Islands of Vanishment conference was designed to cast a wider net, drawing in a mixed haul of architects and tourist operators, members of the community living close to the Port Arthur Historic Site and scholars from other parts of the world, experts in stonework, heritage administrators and many more—people of all kinds who are concerned in one way or another with the what, the why or the how of heritage sites but who are not always able to meet each other and exchange views. So I hope that there were useful encounters of kinds that aren't too wearisomely familiar, and I hope, too, that the question raised by Peter Romey in relation to conservation and tourism—'Can't we still be friends?'—will get an affirmative reply.

The diversity of topics addressed and sites considered as Islands of Vanishment has been, perhaps, even more striking than the opalescent dazzle of the delegates. And the questions which have come flying up in clouds out of the clash of concepts have been more diverse still, especially when one kind of Island of Vanishment has been set against another. For example, as a result of a conversation about escapes, I found myself comparing this prison here at Port Arthur with the kind of prisoner-of-war camp featured in movies like *The Wooden Horse*. And this led me to wonder for the first time how many of the Irish, say, who were held prisoner here saw themselves as engaged in war against England. Or how many transported for ostensibly neutral offences, like stealing livestock, were actually political or politicised prisoners. Or, at the very time when, back in London, Karl Marx was hard at work in the British Museum, how many convicts, from all parts of Britain, could be regarded as prisoners taken in a long-running class war.

One might go on, pointing out for instance, as Phillip Adams has done, that detention centres like Woomera may be termed quite properly concentration camps, which gives rise to interesting questions about the political capital gained by certain leaders of small stature and large ambition when they whip up popular fear and hatred of some unhappy minority.

After only a little of this kind of thing it dawned on me that many Islands of Vanishment have been created out of fear, which can range from the quite proper—if belated—caution of those who finally pinned Napoleon down on St Helena to the murderous paranoia of a Stalin or a Pol Pot. I think one could also say that

Closing speech delivered at The Islands of Vanishment conference, Port Arthur (June 2002)

even when the occupants of certain Islands of Vanishment stayed alive, rather than disappearing for ever into killing fields or mass graves, many such islands have been intended to change the personalities of the inmates or destroy their identity. This kind of vanishment is commonly achieved through uniforms and shaved heads, the substitution of numbers for names, the removal of personal possessions, the restriction of social contacts and, above all, the stifling of the individual voice by depriving the criminal, the alien, the pauper, the ethnically tainted, the ideologically unsound of any means of expression. In fact, many Islands of Vanishment have been first and foremost Islands of Silence.

Some prison reformers, who advocated the use of solitary confinement and the imposition of silence and anonymity through the apparatus of masks, chapel stalls and so on, were men of goodwill. John Howard—like the present-day actor of that name—was certainly well-intentioned. Yet it is no coincidence that Howard's methods found favour in the 1790s at the point where the British Government, alarmed by events in France and the spread of dangerously radical doctrines amongst the newly industrialised working-class, brought in its gagging bills, banning gatherings of more than fifty people and tightening up the law on seditious utterance. More than fifty years before the model prison next door was completed, radical opinion which had supported Howard's program of prison reform turned against the new penitentiaries, denouncing them as 'receptacles for persons who write or speak disagreeable truths'. And yet large numbers of those who have been confined in silent prisons or similar Islands of Vanishment, who were supposed to go unheard or to vanish without trace and be forgotten, are still known to us, either because of the conservation of sites in which they lived or died, or the independent survival of their own testimony, or the existence of someone else's reports, records, stories in which we can still catch glimpses of a living person.

Shakespeare was much concerned with being remembered and in his sonnets made great play with the ancient literary convention of asserting that the written word will outlast memorials of stone or brass. So in a number of the sonnets addressed to the Friend, the beautiful young man who may or may not have been Mr W H, Shakespeare promises that the Friend's beauty will be remembered until the end of time. In sonnet 107, for instance, from which I've borrowed the title of this paper, he scorns 'tombs of brass', telling the young man 'And thou in this shall find thy monument', referring, of course, to the sonnet itself, the 'poore rime' that he has written down in his black ink.

I don't want to engage in a debate over the relative longevity of Shakespeare's sonnets and Stonehenge or even Frank the Poet's 'Ballad of the Cyprus Brig' which was forbidden to be sung—and the stones of this prison in which he was confined. Quite the contrary. I'm not really concerned today with the separate lives of words or walls but more with the way in which the heritage site and the words which have come out of it or which shed light on it are joined as means to one end.

And Islands of Vanishment, particularly when they have been designed as also Islands of Silence, are perhaps special in this regard. When the inmates of such places have somehow managed to express themselves in words or have been given a form of extended life in the testimony of others, the page is not just an important clue to the significance of the abandoned camp or ghetto or gaol but, still more importantly, a powerful reason for conserving that historic site. Of course, we value sites like Port Arthur because to gloss away the cruelty and deprivation of the past is to build an impoverished present on deceit, but I'd suggest we should also value such places as memorials to those who refused to be reduced or silenced. These people should, I believe, find their monuments not just in the page as site but also in the fabrics we conserve.

When one first starts thinking about prison literature it seems that if prisons really have been intended to prevent self-expression and shut people up they haven't worked particularly well. The list of sizeable books, often hugely important, influential books, written in prisons is long. It includes *The Consolations of Philosophy,* written by the sixth-century philosopher Boethius—a work much venerated in the Middle Ages and translated in turn by King Alfred, Chaucer and Queen Elizabeth I—and many of the poems of Sir Walter Raleigh, as well as all he managed to write of his *History of the World.* Raleigh spent years in the Tower of London and was twice condemned to death, a fate he confronts with wit and courage, in a poem called the 'Passionate Man's Pilgrimage'. In fact he didn't die the day after writing this poem but was beheaded, quite unjustly, about fifteen years later. In the poem he imagines his soul travelling to Heaven at his death just as a pilgrim or palmer might travel to the Holy City of Jerusalem. He ends it like this:

> *And this is my eternal plea To him that made heaven earth and sea, Seeing my flesh must die so soon And want a head to dine next noon, Just at the stroke when my veins start and spread Set on my soul an everlasting head. Then am I ready like a palmer fit, To tread those blest paths which before I writ.*

John Bunyan, although he was imprisoned for preaching without a licence, produced nine books of religious instruction during his first gaol term and wrote the first part of *The Pilgrim's Progress* during a later stint. Then there's the Marquis de Sade, who wrote in a rather different vein; the transportees Henry Savery, Australia's first novelist, and the Irish patriot, John Mitchel, who kept a *Jail Journal* but was allowed a measure of freedom in Van Diemen's Land. He wrote:

> *In vain I try to torment myself into a state of chronic savage indignation: it will not do here. In vain I reflect that I am after all, in a real cell, hulk, or dungeon yet—that these woodlands, are but Carthaginian prison walls –that the bright birds, waving their rainbow wings here before me, are but 'ticket-of-leave' birds, and enjoy only 'comparative liberty'—in vain—there is in every soul of man a buoyancy that will not let it sink to utter despair.*

Then there's Frank McNamara or Frank the Poet whose feisty ballads provide a sharp contrast to penitent descriptions of the horrors of Van Diemen's Land, including the ballad of that name, probably commissioned by authority to discourage crime. Later comes Oscar Wilde's *De Profundis,* written in Reading Gaol, and much else including a small book on the trade union law of Sierra Leone written by my late husband, Michael Scott. In the late 1950s when Michael was practising as a barrister in Sierra Leone he rather rashly helped bail one of his clients, a diamond smuggler called Lazarovich. Unfortunately, Lazarovich attempted to leave Sierra Leone and was caught with more diamonds secreted in a private part of his anatomy. Not surprisingly, the police concluded that Michael was in cahoots with Lazarovich and promptly put him in gaol, where, being of a philosophical temperament, he settled down to write his book. In the preface he thanks various people who have assisted him in his work including the Extra-Mural Department of Fourah Bay College. He also thanks the Government of Sierra Leone 'for financing a period of leisure and retirement during which it was possible to complete my work'.

There are also, of course, hundreds of books written by prisoners after their escape or release in which they describe their time in Siberian gulags or Japanese prisoner-of-war camps or other sites of incarceration. And there are a few, like the *Diary of Anne Frank*, left to us by those who afterwards vanished, which deal with a victim's earlier experience.

Many of these writings are valuable historical documents providing details about sites we may wish to conserve; virtually all are themselves strong reasons for that conservation. If, for instance, it should ever be decided that the Tower of London ought to be bulldozed to make way for a shopping mall, I hope some protester will arise waving in his or her hand a copy of Raleigh's 'Passionate Man's Pilgrimage'.

Raleigh and other prison-writers before and after him rejected 'utter stark despair' and wrote with the odds against them. There are, of course, millions of others who were more effectively silenced but who have managed to leave some hint of their personalities, their individual voices behind. And I want to end today by saluting three of these. The first is a man with the rather odd name of Kyd Wake, an English printer, who, like Denis Collins, had a grudge against his king. Wake, however, threw no stone. He merely hissed and booed the royal carriage for which, in 1796, he was sentenced to five years' hard labour. He was sent to Gloucester Gaol, one of the new penitentiaries where prisoners were kept in solitary confinement and subjected to a discipline similar to that of our Model Prison—though not quite so rigid since Wake's wife was allowed to send him extra food. In order to raise money for purchasing the food, Mrs Wake had an engraving made of her husband, dressed in prison uniform and standing in his cell, which she sold to the citizens of Gloucester. Underneath the engraving was printed Kyd Wake's own description of 'the horrors of solitary imprisonment under penitentiary discipline'. The passage ends with the reflection that if

> *Judges and Jurors would but consider what an irreparable misfortune it is to have a considerable portion of life so wearisomely wasted, they would surely be more tender of dooming any man, for a long time, to such wretchedness. It is a calamity beyond description, more easily to be conceived than explained.*

The next voice out of the silence belongs to Thomas Walker, who was transported to Van Diemen's Land at the age of sixteen for housebreaking. From the moment of his arrival in Van Diemen's Land in September 1824, Walker was a thorn in authority's side largely because he was absolutely determined to escape. His record shows that he made one attempt after another, twice managing to hide away on ships. He was savagely punished, receiving over a thousand lashes before he made his last and most spectacular escape attempt in 1839. It was actually an escape rather than an escape attempt because Walker with seven companions got clean away from Port Arthur in Commandant Booth's Whale Boat and was at large for over three months. I'd like to dwell on the events of that time since they demonstrate that Walker, as well as being a remarkable leader and strategist, had somehow remained a humane and humorous human being despite the treatment he'd received. But I'll have to confine myself to bits of a deposition provided by a Mr Davis of George's River on the east coast of Tasmania. Walker and his men lived, of course, by raiding settlements and taking what they needed, but they always left settlers with enough to eat and only once discharged a firearm in the course of a raid. The part of the escapees' story I like best concerns Walker's arrival at the Davis property, smartly dressed in stolen clothes, clearly in charge of the Whale Boat crew and, telling Mr Davis that he was out hunting for the Walker gang. Davis cordially invited him to dinner—which was duly eaten—and even after the ruse had been discovered, went on to defend the remarkable Walker as far as he possibly could. In his deposition Davis insists that Walker and his men treated him with the greatest respect, civility and attention.

Lastly comes Renee Friesova, who as a Jewish teenager living in Czechoslovakia was sent with her parents to Terezin, a concentration camp which was not itself a death camp—though many died there from hunger, overcrowding or disease—but was a feeder-camp for Auschwitz, so that regularly many of those Renee knew—her friends, her teachers—disappeared never to be seen again. Renee not only managed to preserve her own identity and her own voice during her imprisonment but in her book *Fortress of My Youth* also pays tribute to others who did the same. She writes:

'The German authorities strictly forbade teaching. Even though the plan for the final solution of the Jewish question was being implemented, what would happen if some of the Jews survived? The Germans did not want the Jews to be educated.'

The SS searched the camp for pencils, books and paper but failed to prevent dedicated teachers from working with the young late in the evenings, preserving their ability to use language as Renee, one of the few to survive, has done to remarkable effect. She also pays tribute to her fellow prisoners' love of music, telling how they smuggled instruments into the camp and even secretly performed operas, though productions were constantly disrupted when members of the cast vanished on the transports to Auschwitz. I don't know if Terezin has become a heritage site—I hope so and I also hope that it is not simply a place of mourning but also one which celebrates the voices which refused, so courageously, to be silenced.

I also hope that we who are privileged—who have liberty, books, writing materials and all kinds of technological wizardry—will go on working to preserve both sites and words which are not just sad memorials to the vanished but also celebrations of those who refused to be crushed or who are struggling now for their right to be heard. I hope that in what we write and what we conserve they will find their monument.

Love letters

I fell in love with Margaret long before I met her. Years—decades—ago I used to edit an American scholarly journal. One day an essay arrived from Tasmania, twelve pages long, typed on a manual typewriter. It was on marriage contracts in *Measure for Measure*—not a natural subject for a tour de force—and it was brilliant. I was an instant fan. 'Who are you,' said my letter of acceptance; 'where is Tasmania; why do you live there?'

The carefully handwritten reply, a tiny autobiography, made us best friends for life. That was the only prompt response I've ever had from Margaret: she is a terrible correspondent, which is all the worse because the letters, when they finally do arrive, are treasures.

We finally met a couple of years later, in 1983: I was at the ANU's Humanities Centre in Canberra. Margaret had arranged a lecture for me at the University of Tasmania, and Hobart was my first view of the rest of Australia. Hardly anybody came to the lecture, but the hospitality she and her colleagues provided was overwhelming, including an insanely funny group expedition to Lake Pedder.

Margaret's conversation was magical. My journal, alas, records almost none of it. At that time Margaret's poetry was hard to come by—there were only a couple of slim volumes, *Visited* and *Tricks of Memory,* shyly offered as I left; but these alone convinced me that a major poet was hiding out in Tasmania.

Three years later, in Hobart again, I was suddenly, mysteriously, a celebrity—the audience for my lecture this time included both the governor and the archbishop—and Margaret gave a superlative dinner for eight of us, cooked by her son Daniel, over which, in between completely unnecessary bouts of nervousness that Daniel would produce something 'peculiar', she recounted, hilariously, fragments of her youth. I did record several of these, but all of them are ones she herself recounts in *Changing Countries.* A pity: how I would have loved to be the diarist who preserved for the world that stroke of baffling, zany genius on her Cambridge entrance exam, 'The relation between gender and case is not fortuitous.'

The best thing about my wonderful last visit to Tasmania, in 1993, was being settled in the drawing room at Tara with the unfinished manuscript of *Family Album,* then titled *The Brown Photograph,* much of it a first draft in her patient, precise script. I was fascinated, and we discussed it endlessly, for days. The ingenuity of the conception was such, however, that meddling with it was irresistible. I had a number of suggestions for changes and elaborations, all of which, fortunately, she ignored, to produce that amazing novel.

'Those evenings come back to me with a mocking radiance'—Edith Wharton, recalling her friendship with Henry James in two exquisite chapters of her memoir *A Backward Glance,* despairs of reconstructing the magic of their meetings. Fortunately I can still write Margaret love letters. This is one. Margaret, I adore you.

Stephen Orgel
J E Reynolds Professor in Humanities
Department of English Stanford University, Stanford

Ageing

As Western culture grows more and more obsessed with youth and staying young, the over-sixties are increasingly despised, elbowed aside and expected to become invisible. We are, it seems, conditioned to think of later life as a state separated off from the rest of our time on earth, a region beyond the pale, inhabited by people who are 'them' not 'us': wrinklies, oldies, incontinent, demented geriatrics who, in crossing the line into the dreadful wasteland of old age, yield up any beauty, brains, character, strength, sexuality, talent, value or purpose they may happen to have carried up to the frontier. Only a fortunate few who have managed to retain a youthful look, like Cher or Tina Turner, or who enjoy unusual power or prestige escape this fate, allowed to linger behind in the land of the young as illegal immigrants until eventually they are accepted as icons or national treasures like Nelson Mandela or the Queen Mother.

The technological cyclone has ripped away the importance which once belonged to older people as story tellers and custodians of tribal lore, as repositories of essential knowledge and transmitters of wisdom. Even the word 'wisdom' has dropped out of the English language as it is used by most speakers other than the usual galactic adventurers and a few lingering hobbits. In Australia, despite the traditional respect for age associated with some ethnic communities and with indigenous culture, the determination to keep the old out of sight and, if possible, out of mind is particularly strong.

One reason for this lies in the national obsession with just about any kind of sport. Every winter is dominated by the footy, every summer by Test cricket, and the year 2000 by the once-in-a-lifetime thrills of the Sydney Olympics. Women participate in their own high-level competitions, occasionally winning spectacular fame as individual athletes, but so far as I know, nobody continues to cut the mustard as a first-class sports person much beyond the age of forty—proving yet again that the aged are irrelevant to the central concerns of modern life. Instead, the sports that attract the biggest television audiences and the biggest money are team games played by an elite made up entirely of young men. Much of the sport watched in Australia is, then, sexist and all that is widely popular is ageist.

Of course, the refusal to acknowledge the existence of the aged may, in the end, have less to do with contempt induced by their physical shortcomings and more with terror induced by the thought of footing the bill for their maintenance in the future. The old are growing rapidly in numbers. Unaware of their irrelevance and uselessness they are living on for ever-increasing periods, so that, all over the Western world, the cohorts of those past the usual retirement age are getting larger in comparison with young populations of workers. In Australia, there are already nearly three million men and women who are over sixty, the age at which they can qualify as card-carrying seniors. Soon, as the baby-boomers achieve seniority, the over-sixties will make up close to a third of the Australian population. Nobody

From a work in progress, extracted in The Best Australian Essays 2001 knows exactly how many will turn out to be superannuants or self-funded retirees, but given the absence of a national superannuation scheme before 1986 and the shift away from full-time employment and uninterrupted saving over the last two decades, the number is likely to be disturbingly low.

Figures relating to women, who live on average longer than men but have less financial independence, are particularly unpromising. Not so long ago 9 per cent of Australian women over fifty-five years of age proved to have superannuation accounts, many of which were hopelessly small because of time taken off work to raise families. Australia's age pensions are not over-generous, its health insurance scheme has been starved of funds and its provision of public funding for aged-care facilities is manifestly inadequate, yet before long the cost of maintaining even the current levels of support for the swelling ranks of the elderly will blow out with an apocalyptic roar. Either taxes, paid mostly by those in work, will shoot up into the stratosphere or the whole tottering structure of state welfare will collapse—unless, of course, some way out of the impasse can be found in the nick of time. No wonder the children of the baby-boomers, brought up when self-interest had already been inflated into a virtue, are reluctant to face up to any reminder of the approaching horde of geriatric users who are going to look to them to do the paying.

As so often happens when you take too long over writing about a hot topic, circumstances have changed since I put together my introductory chapter. The old, for instance, are more visible than they used to be. Elderly faces, especially female ones, are still rarely seen on television, unless they belong to the comically dotty or those who are lying dying in hospital soapies, but nursing home scandals have become big news. So too have the clashes between Federal and State governments as they circle around in preparation for a long war, trying to mark out the limits of their respective responsibilities for aged care.

Forced to pay attention to the escalating number of seniors in this country, the Howard government has suddenly woken up to the importance of grey power in an election year, and has started throwing large amounts of money at self-funded retirees and small amounts at age pensioners in an attempt to buy their votes. The scheme has been widely publicised, ostensibly to inform older Australians of 'their entitlements', but has not been received with quite as much enthusiasm as the Prime Minister might have wished. The nature of the over-sixty cohort seems already to be changing, becoming less meek, more demanding and more insistent on becoming visible than ever before.

With Margaret the style is ever love

I remember many years ago Margaret came to visit me in Oxford. We passed a rather pleasant afternoon drinking. As the sun sank low over the playing fields behind my rooms, I recounted to her how a psychologist student friend had told me I drank too much coffee, and that coffee destroyed beta level brain activity, which, he had said, was the creative aspect of the mind.

Margaret, a woman given to defending the necessity of folly and the splendour of vice, held a guttering Stuyvo in one hand and a near-empty glass of Bulgarian Bull's Blood—a red wine popular with Oxford students of the day on the basis of price, if not taste—in the other.

It was clear to me that Margaret did not take well this news of the artistic cost of coffee. Lighting a new fag off the long ash stick of her old still-smouldering smoke, she rolled those great mischievous eyes in a wicked twirl, like old gramophone 78s being spun in some lost interwar moonlight, sighed, and then said, in a manner that would brook no further argument: 'Bloody Balzac died of caffeine poisoning.'

Large-hearted, acid-witted, witch-cackling, piss-taking, self-deprecating, story-telling Margaret Scott. I recall her tale of how when studying at Cambridge in the 1950s she joined a bohemian push that included Sylvia Plath and Ted Hughes. Ted Hughes marvelled at the smallness of Margaret's feet. Soon after that he ditched a friend of Margaret's for Sylvia Plath at the now famous St Botolph's Review party of 3 March, 1956, 'though no one, she says, holds her miniscule feet responsible for this seismic literary coupling. The girlfriend came up to Margaret in the course of that evening and said: 'Ted just kissed that American girl.' 'With what seems to have been an unusually reliable capacity for reaching the wrong conclusion,' Margaret told me, 'I assured her the kiss meant nothing.' Thus Margaret dismissed what was to be the most famous literary romance of the twentieth century.

Years ago I stood before Margaret Scott, which was for me, though not the more venerable Margaret, half a lifetime ago. Then, as now, I stood with a few pieces of paper upon which were penned some ill-conceived, worse-written thoughts clutched in my sweating hand; then, as today, terrified, nervous, hoping that these words might meet with Margaret's approval.

The pieces of paper then were my first-ever short stories, which I had taken to Margaret for her considered opinion. And that day, in her book-hillocked, amber-hued university office, her face half-illuminated in a cone of falling yellow light, half-dissolving in the swirls of rising smoke, she did something remarkable. She made me feel I was a real writer. My stories, I can now confess, were terrible. As Margaret pored over them, cigarette inevitably in raised hand, the scrim of fine ash settling on those awful pages could not hide from her acute eye the malign influence of de Maupassant, the structural shortcomings, the stylistic excesses, the myriad failings, but somehow she managed to make me think two things: that I needed to do much, much more work, but that nevertheless my writing was worth-while and that I ought persevere.

As I was leaving, Margaret handed me a volume of her poems, entitled *Tricks of Memory,* and she inscribed it to me. Margaret's advice left me buoyed, determined, and her kindness and wisdom I felt was embodied in that book of poems she gave me. It was a small book and to me it looked and felt like a passport into a new country in which I had for so long wished to live: the republic of letters. It was at that moment, I suspect, that I became a writer. That small book I took with me everywhere I went thereafter. I have it here with me this afternoon, a little like its author, a little older, slightly marinaded in wine, coffee and memories, and still marvellous. Margaret gave writers here not only a sense that we should write, but the belief that this world, our world here in Tasmania, was a fit one for literature, and she connected this country of Tasmania through the experience of her own life with the other place to which all writers belong, the infinite universe of books. If there is something remarkable happening in Tasmanian writing now, something large, generous and extraordinary, I suspect it is perhaps Margaret's spirit writ large. Of course, none of this, at the end of the day, means that much. I came to know Margaret over many years through the best, and also the worst, of times.

We all feel how much we owe Margaret. But more, moreover. How much we love her. Chekhov said style is the man. With Margaret the style is ever love.

Richard Flanagan
Writer

Lizzie and the great outdoors

The back garden was very small and bounded on three sides by high walls topped by little wooden fences. Along the narrow fencetops cats would suddenly come stalking, small tigers in the sky, remote and alien as clouds or shadows passing smoothly behind glass. Lizzie watched them sometimes when she was playing in the corner by the coalhouse wall—but would no more have thought of trying to waylay one of these passers-by than of reaching up to halt the stars in their courses.

Her world was in the earth, especially the big shady bed of dark loam where the French beans swarmed upwards over a rampart of tall sticks, embellishing the air with green curlicues and scarlet flowers. Along the front of the bed was a row of heavy stones leaning uphill to divide the banked soil from the lawn. And here between two stones Mowgli had his house. The roof was made of a little piece of polished wood that might have been sawn from an architrave. It was a dark mottled chestnut colour, curved and very smooth. Under this lid Mowgli could sleep contentedly on a bed of grass clippings among his spears and stores of berries with a tiny saucepan, brought from the dolls' house, nestling among his neatly piled firewood.

Mowgli was made of felt, thin, pliant and orangey-brown. He had begun as a six-inch fairy doll with flaxen hair, gauze skirt and wand. Stripped little by little of every ornament except his white underpants he had changed his sex and embarked on a new life in the great outdoors. In Lizzie's hand or suspended from a bit of cotton he bounced across the lawn, scaled the buddleia, hunted beetles, woodlice and ants, and gathered fragments of petal and leaf for his salads. Yet he was much more than a puppet. The big staring dolls who sat in a schoolroom row at the top of the house, waiting to be smacked and ordered about on rainy days, offered puny little Lizzie the pleasure of absolute power over their existence. Mowgli did something different. He was the agent of creation through whom the meticulously tended little garden became a wild exotic world of great plains, trees with spikes of purple bloom as long and thick as a man's body, and strange groves hung with shining scarlet fruit bigger than giant pumpkins. There were structures here more gigantic, more mysterious than the pyramids, more wonderful than anything in the ruined city of *The Jungle Book:* cliffs of enormous bricks; a pair of terracotta urns spilling leaves the size of tea-trays and blossoms as big as human heads; highways of room-sized slabs of smooth stone; and a vast cavern, like a cathedral, filled with slopes of glossy black boulders rising into the distant cobwebby darkness.

As well as all this, Mowgli was the means by which Lizzie herself was created anew, not just because she controlled his every action but because together they performed amazing, death-defying physical feats. Lizzie, in the ordinary way, was a bony little thing, always ailing, and, although she passionately longed to be a boy, hopeless at climbing trees or catching balls. But Mowgli could leap from a standing position to halfway up the buddleia tree and then, without even a swinging vine to help him, cross in one great agile bound to the French beans. He was never tired, never ill and, when he fell from some enormous height, never harmed. If he got wet on a night of rain when snails crawled into his house and stuck themselves to his ceiling he could be dried out in the morning. If he got muddy he could be washed and if his arm got torn, as it once did when he was prising thorns for arrow heads off a rose bush, he simply went into a trance until he had been sewn together with neat orange stitches.

The only real danger that Lizzie and Mowgli faced came in the form of invading giants who sometimes clumped down the steps from the cement ramp by the garage, round the circular bed and on to their grass. Lizzie's mother occasionally set about digging daisies out of the lawn with a special fork or carted a deckchair down from the garage to sit and sew in the sun. But she, though sometimes puzzled and anxious, was the least intrusive of the invaders. It was quite possible for Mowgli to flit to some point out of her line of vision and for Lizzie to hunch herself up in a small cone of concentration where, so long as she remembered not to speak aloud, she was quite safe.

The story of Mowgli's adventurous afternoon could spin on in silence, his actions matching the words that ran through Lizzie's head:

'One day Mowgli decided to go out to the Great Prickle Tree beyond the Big Rocks to collect some spiky needles for knitting a cloak and for skewers in his meat. He took some apples for his dinner wrapped up in a cloth tied to his belt. He took a big stick and set out without a care in the world. He climbed the rocks beside his house and made his way along the Big Brown Plain to the place where he could jump down to the lovely soft grass by the Prickle Tree. He knew he must be very careful because the prickles were deadly poison—no—the prickles were very sharp. "Ha! Ha!" he said. "I should have brought my sack …"'

'What's that dear?'

'Nothing,' said Lizzie crossly. 'I didn't say anything.'

'You said something about a sack.'

Lizzie kept quite still, biting her lip and viciously nipping spines from the little conifer that, every year, was dug up, put in a pot and hung with fairy lights.

'Was it part of your game?'

'I was just making up a story about a Christmas tree.' 'Oh! Father Christmas's sack!'

Lizzie didn't bother to reply. She stared at Mowgli, fidgeting him backwards and forwards until the stupid clumsy pretence of Father Christmas had slunk away and the delicate magic of the prickle-hunt had restored itself.

'I wonder if these soft green needles are good to eat,' he said. 'Mmm! They're sweet as sugar cane. I'll make a bundle and tie it with my string. I always carry string in my dinner bag and my pink knife I made from a piece of shell. These other stiff old needles will make good skewers. I wonder if I could find some really long ones to make arrows for my bow.' And with this Mowgli whipped out his trusty knife and began to cut lots of big needles from the Great Prickle Tree.

Lizzie's mother sighed. She was glad in a way that Lizzie was so well-behaved, never wanting to run off and play in the street, but she worried over the way she kept to herself all the time. It must come, she thought, of being so delicate and having to spend all those weeks shut away in a sick room when she was tiny.

But Lizzie's father was less easygoing. He complained about flowers nipped from his tomato plants and he didn't like Mowgli's house being where it was. He thought it looked untidy—that bit of wood stuck in his neat row of stones. People must wonder, he said to Lizzie's mother, when they came to look at his beans. When he got up on the bed to attend to his framework of sticks he carefully avoided looking at his feet as though, it seemed to Lizzie, he wouldn't have been sorry if, apparently by mistake, he'd stepped back on Mowgli's house and crushed it.

One day Mr Cheshire from next-door was invited to inspect the crop. Mr Cheshire was a natty widower in his early forties with patent-leather hair and a flat moustache. He had a housekeeper who cooked his meals and cleaned his house, a car and a good job at Filton aeroplane works. Lizzie's mother had an idea that he'd fallen in love with her younger sister, Virgie, so whenever Virgie came to supper Lizzie's mother got out the Crown Derby dinner service, cooked something special, and asked Mr Cheshire to call round at about seven.

'He's a good catch,' she told her sister as they bustled about together getting the meal.

Virgie, who wore perky hats, high heels and very red lipstick, tossed her head. She was still getting letters from an American lieutenant she'd met at a dance.

'He's not as good-looking as Artie,' she said, but when Mr Cheshire came out into the kitchen on his way to look over the beans she turned the colour of the tomatoes she'd sliced to arrange on the salad in its cutglass bowl.

Out in the garden Mr Cheshire caught sight of Mowgli's roof, picked it up and waggled it about in a rallying sort of way.

'Been doing a bit of woodwork, Ted?'

This for Lizzie's father was the last straw. He scooped up Mowgli and the saucepan, dropped them on the coalhouse window-sill and brushed away all Mowgli's household supplies with his fingertips.

'Some mess of Lizzie's,' he said and shied the roof into the kindling box just inside the coalhouse door.

When Lizzie went out into the garden after school next day, she couldn't believe her eyes. At first she thought of throwing herself on the grass and screaming until she made herself ill. She pictured her mother running out, her father carrying her up to bed, her own face all hot and teary against her pillow, and Dr Merchant sitting on the bed, taking her pulse.

'Daddy broke my house,' she'd tell them, still sobbing. And her mother and the doctor would turn and stare accusingly at her father. But the more she thought of all this, the more frightened she became at the prospect of such an enormous upset. When she pictured her mother's rage against her father she began to feel quite sorry for him.

'I ask you,' her mother would say, 'I ask you what harm was the child doing? Don't try to get round me with your excuses. It's self, self, self with you, Ted, and

I'm sick, weary and tired of it…'

So Lizzie started making a new house for Mowgli in the rockery. She dug out a neat rectangle in the slope near one of the rocks and lined the inside walls with small stones pressed into the earth. The front of the house was left open so that Mowgli could get a view of his whole kingdom. When Lizzie rescued his roof from the kindling box and put it in place it was clear that the new dwelling was far finer as well as safer than the old one.

Since it was nearly suppertime by now Mowgli had to get his bedding together very quickly. Tomorrow would be a busy day with fresh supplies of food and fuel to be gathered …

Meanwhile, pausing over his tripe and onions, Lizzie's father said, 'So when are we going to hear these wedding bells?'

'You can laugh,' said Lizzie's mother, 'but he'll ask her sure as eggs, believe you me.'

Virgie began coming round for supper more often than before. Lizzie didn't like her much even though it was she who had given Lizzie the fairy doll from whom Mowgli had emerged like a butterfly from a lifeless-looking chrysalis. Virgie was mad about clothes and hair, always criticising the way Lizzie looked, always jerking at her hems and tweaking at her sleeves.

'Oh Peg! You can't let her go about in that old thing!'; 'Why don't you put a bit of a curl in her hair? It's like a yard of pump water!'; 'Why don't you get her something with a nice puffed sleeve?'

Fortunately Virgie was too busy nowadays to bother much with Lizzie any more. She spent all her time talking to Lizzie's mother about the two men in her life and, when she and Peg were settled side by side in the back garden, she forgot completely that Lizzie was even there. But Lizzie, entranced for the first time by what Aunty Virgie had to say to her mother, often found tasks for Mowgli that took her close up behind the two deckchairs. While Mowgli gathered grass for his bed or tore up daisy leaves, Lizzie would squat in the chairs' shadow, quiet as a mouse, willing Aunty Virgie to stay true to handsome Artie Schwartz. It was rather as though Virgie had two separate existences like a film star—one in the everyday world where she went on being her ordinary bossy self, the other up in the silvery realm of romance where she became the heroine you longed to see living happily ever after with a hero far more dashing than Mr Cheshire.

Sometimes the duel being played out between Virgie's two lovers became so intense that Mowgli dropped from Lizzie's hand and, overcome by unaccustomed lethargy, fell asleep, unheeded, in the shade of Virgie's deckchair.

'Of course, Artie's very romantic. Everyone says he's the image of Alan Ladd.'

'You can't live on romance, Virgo. You've got to think. You don't even know if he's got a job to go back to.'

'He used to run this drugstore. I told you. In this little town in Oregon.'

'Drugstore? What, a chemist's like Boots or something? Does he own the shop himself?'

'I think so. He's not short of money, Peg.'

'But you don't know what this drugstore place amounts to. It could be just some one-eyed little shop. You could get out there and find yourself dishing out syrup of figs until you drop.'

'Oh, I don't think Artie would let me work.'

'They can say anything they like while they're over here. Make out they'll give you the world when all the time they haven't got tuppence. But you know where you are with Mr Cheshire. You'd have that car and everything. And he'll always have that job according to Ted. It's not just for the duration like a lot of them in munitions…'

'But Artie's so generous!'

'Generous now he's got money to throw about. What about when the war's over and you're out there in this Oregon and it turns out he hasn't got the price of a hot meal? What about that?'

Despite all Artie's virtues, Virgie started going about with Mr Cheshire in his car. They went to the pictures to see *Gone With The Wind*, after which Virgie admitted that Mr Cheshire looked a bit like Clark Gable. She went next door to admire his golfing trophies, was shown over the house and introduced to the Welsh housekeeper, Mrs Evans, who served up tea and rock-cakes in the dining room.

'You drink that while it's hot,' said Mrs Evans to Mr Cheshire.

'I will, I will. Don't I always do as I'm told like a good boy?'

Mr Cheshire thought this was a great joke and winked at Virgie but afterwards Virgie told Lizzie's mother that Mrs Evans was an old dragon.

'If I ever did—you know—I wouldn't keep her on for five minutes.'

'Well, he wouldn't expect to have a housekeeper once he was married again.'

'Oh, I'd want someone. With him bringing in all that money I'm not getting down on my knees scrubbing floors. But I couldn't put up with her. Nasty old biddy, bossing him about. Her and her cats. They're the ones that get up on the fence, you know. I'd complain about it if I were you.'

Even after things had advanced to this stage Virgie still went on at times about Artie. She couldn't resist the pleasure of pirouetting for just a little longer high on the peak of her eternal triangle. This was her way of enjoying a last fling before she settled down to married life. And she didn't want anyone to run away with the idea that Bill Cheshire could have her just for the asking, although she hadn't actually told Bill himself that he had a rival. Being so much older, Bill was inclined to be jealous and was always saying how disgusting it was to see British girls making themselves cheap with the Yanks. So Virgie had to make do with teasing her sister and her girlfriends in the typing pool where she worked.

'It's really Artie I love,' she'd sigh. 'In my heart he's still king.'

But after a while nobody except Lizzie believed her.

In July, about a month before VJ Day, something terrible happened. One Saturday afternoon Virgie got up from her deckchair so quickly that Lizzie barely had time to scuttle back a few yards before her aunt turned round and saw her. Mowgli was left lying on the lawn. Virgie caught sight of him, snatched him up and went pink with indignation.

'This is that lovely little doll I gave you for Christmas! Look, Peg, what she's done! Pulled off all the little clothes and all the hair and everything! Destructive little monkey!'

'She still plays with it though, Virgo. It's her favourite, isn't it dear?'

'Well, I s'pose I could fix it. Not that she deserves it, mind you.'

And to Lizzie's horror Virgie opened her big shiny handbag, tossed Mowgli down among the lipsticks and hairpins and snapped the bag shut.

'You don't need to bother,' said Lizzie's mother. 'She likes it as it is.'

'Nobody could like it like that. What, is she daft or something?'

Lizzie crept to her mother, gripped her arm and looked up, imploringly at her face. But Peg only smiled weakly and tried to avoid Lizzie's eye. She wanted her daughter to be a nice normal little girl. She wasn't going to do anything more to convince Virgie that Lizzie had an unnatural taste in dolls.

Lizzie felt quite sick. She thought again of starting a screaming fit but saw at once, where everyone would understand her being upset over a broken toy, nobody was going to understand why she didn't want one mended. There was nothing to be done. She had to watch Mowgli carted away in his swinging prison to be twisted and turned in Virgie's fingers with their long red nails, stabbed with needles and changed back into a namby-pamby thing that couldn't throw a spear to save its life.

She had one last quick glimpse of Mowgli before he was taken away to Aunty Virgie's house. When the deckchairs had been stowed away, Virgie took out an envelope of photographs that Artie had sent her from Berlin. She giggled in an 'aren't I awful' kind of way as she spread them out on the table for Peg to see.

'Just look at that profile, will you!'

She gazed at it with her head on one side.

'You ought to write,' said Lizzie's mother shortly.

'Oh, yes, well, all in good time.'

Still giggling, Virgie packed up the photos and pushed them back into her bag. Lizzie, leaning close, spotted Mowgli's orange leg sticking up from under Artie's envelope. The transformation happened very quickly. Three days later Mowgli came back, totally restored as Fairy Twinkletoes and wrapped in white tissue paper. Virgie unveiled him proudly on the kitchen table.

'Look!' she said. 'I even put a little star on the wand!'

Lizzie thanked her in a dull voice and took Mowgli upstairs. She was determined to rescue him from all his feminine encumbrances as soon as she could but when she looked at him closely she saw that Virgie had done a much better job than the commercial maker who'd put the fairy doll together in the first place. This time Mowgli's white bodice was sewn to his skin around the neck and armholes and his blond hair, instead of being stuck on with a dab of glue, was embroidered into his scalp. It was going to be very difficult to cut him loose without mangling him in the process Worst of all, he seemed to accept his renovation quite placidly as though he was really glad to be a fairy again and his wild, free spirit had fled away forever.

Lizzie moped for days, refusing to play in the garden and looking so forlorn that when she finally asked her mother to make her a new Mowgli doll, Peg gave in at once.

'Just don't let Aunty Virgie see it,' she said. 'We don't want to hurt her feelings.'

The felt they bought was a better colour than Old Mowgli's skin—tan rather than orange—and Lizzie's mother went to a lot of trouble in giving New Mowgli a fine head of short black curls made with French knots.

'You could call him Little Sambo,' she said.

But Lizzie pretended not to hear this. She took New Mowgli off to introduce him to his territory and had a wonderful time getting to know his strengths and weaknesses as he went about exploring plain and jungle. He had more stuffing than Old Mowgli, who'd been almost totally flat, so that he had trouble squeezing between rocks.

On the other hand, if his feet were properly wedged, his stiffness made it easy for him to stand without flopping over. After going right round the garden together, Lizzie and New Mowgli called in at the home in the rockery, then bounded off past the mint bed to inspect the coalhouse.

But here New Mowgli's tour ended abruptly.

To Lizzie's great astonishment she found that Lucky, one of Mrs Evans's cats from next door, had come down from the fencetop, settled herself in the kindling box and produced a litter of squirming black kittens. Lizzie ran at once to tell her mother and Mrs Evans who came hurrying round with a basket lined with flannel to take the kittens home to Mr Cheshire's house. Lizzie knelt beside the old woman, peeping sideways at the crinkles in her neck and helping to lift the kittens out of the box.

'Aunty Virgie doesn't like cats,' said Lizzie.

Mrs Evans looked put out.

'Is that right? Well, I dare say she'll come round. Everyone likes my Lucky when they get to know her.'

Lizzie pondered this for a few moments.

'But Auntie Virgie won't get to know her. She isn't going to marry Mr Cheshire.'

'Is that right?' said Mrs Evans again, turning to stare at Lizzie. 'I heard it was just about settled.'

'Oh no. She loves Artie. In her heart he's still king.'

'Artie? Who's that?'

'Artie's an American soldier. He runs a drugstore in a place called Oregon. He's not there now though, because he's been in the war. He's in Berlin. The other day he sent Auntie Virgie all these photos of him and his friends standing in the bomb damage.'

Mrs Evans seemed tickled to death by this news. She pinched Lizzie's cheek and told her she must come next door to play with the kittens when they had their eyes open. Then she put Lucky under one arm and the basket under the other and went off home even more quickly than she'd arrived.

That evening there was a dreadful uproar in the kitchen.

'You must've let something slip,' Virgie shouted at Peg.

'I never did! How can you think such a thing?' Virgie slumped on to a chair and hid her face in her hands. She'd told a whole lot of girls about Artie and they in turn could have told dozens of people. Bill might have heard the story from anybody—someone's boyfriend he'd met at work or someone's mother who'd served him in a shop. She thought of the posters plastered all over the place throughout the war, CARELESS TALK COSTS LIVES and burst into tears.

Months later a batch of wedding photographs arrived from Oregon, followed by a string of breezily cheerful postcards. Then more photos—Artie and Virgie in the new Buick; Artie and Virgie on vacation in Florida; Virgie posed on some steps in her new fur coat…

Lizzie got hold of Fairy Twinkletoes, chopped her skirt to kneelength, took away her wand, pulled off the star and gave the silver stick to new Mowgli. Then she took her out to the garden to be New Mowgli's wife. In this role the poor thing led a wretched life. She had to carry the sack whenever New Mowgli went out foraging, gather the firewood, make the bed and cook all the food.

At nightfall New Mowgli would come back to his house and shout, 'Where are you, stupid Mrs Virgie? Where's my supper? Bring it here this minute you selfish thing! It's self, self, self with you and I'm sick, weary and tired of it!'

And if Mrs Virgie failed to serve up something tasty New Mowgli would wallop her with his wand like Mr Punch in the Punch and Judy show Lizzie had seen once on the sands at Weston-super-Mare.

But the following year, when Lizzie was nearly nine years old, Virgie sent her sister a frantic letter. It turned out that after Artie's business had gone bust he'd run away with Betty-Jo who'd worked in his drugstore, dispensing, to Lizzie's mother's surprise, not syrup of figs but coke and ice-cream sodas.

'She can't say I didn't warn her,' said Peg grimly. 'Alan Ladd, my foot.'

After that Mowgli suddenly became a more considerate husband. He kissed Mrs Virgie on both cheeks and gathered her a great bouquet of scarlet blossoms, picked from the curling tendrils of Lizzie's father's beans as they reached towards the sky by the buddleia tree.

The badger

When I was about six I told terrible lies. Usually this was because people asked me questions to which I didn't know the answers. For instance, at school one day, a big girl with wiry hair called Josephine Shillabeer, said, 'My mother is thirty-two. How old is yours?'

My mother, who was born in the nineteenth century and belonged to a secretive generation, always answered questions about her age by saying, 'I'm as old as my little finger and a little older than my teeth'. I thought about trying this on Josephine but decided against it. She was a very modern girl with small, hard, hazel eyes. So I said, 'My mother is twenty-one'. Actually, at the time, she was forty-eight but I had no way of knowing that. Twenty-one seemed a good age to choose. It was safely adult and connected in some way with parties.

Josephine was put out by this crisp response. We were sitting with our reading books at a low, green-painted table. She looked darkly at a picture of Spot the dog running to Ann and Peter. Then she began to nudge the girl sitting next to her. They whispered and shot me glances laden with doubt and derision. When Miss Northcote came round to see how we were getting on, Josephine waylaid her:

'Margaret Russell says her mother is twenty-one.'

Miss Northcote went red. She took me off to the other end of the room and tried to explain. 'I don't think that can be quite right. I mean, goodness me, she would only have been fifteen when you were born.'

'Yes,' I said.

'No,' said Miss Northcote, getting redder than ever. 'No, I don't think so.'

By now I really believed what I had said. I started to cry. I cried all the way home and wailed as I stumbled in through the back door, 'They won't believe me! They won't believe you're twenty-one!'

This created a crisis. My mother wasn't quite sure whether I'd been loyally asserting her eternal youth or blackening her character. In the end she took a rather sour view of the situation. This was because she was already worried about the way I treated the truth, especially when it came to the question of flying.

The flying bothered her a lot. If she were still alive it might be some comfort to her to know that after all these years it still bothers me. At the time I was quite sure that I could fly. Looking back, I think I can remember taking off, except, of course, that it couldn't have happened.

It couldn't have happened but it seems as though it did. I remember it more clearly than school or Christmases, more clearly even than meeting the badger that early afternoon in Limerick Road.

Flying was strenuous. I used to lie on the dining room floor with my nose in the carpet and take a series of big, gulping breaths. Then I would hold my breath and, inflated like a small balloon, rise slowly from the floor and hover about among the furniture, looking, I imagine, very like a miniature gunship in a green serge gym slip. I had to hold my breath the whole time, so the flights were always short, but at least once I skimmed out into the hall and made a quick circuit over the patterned tiles. On bumping gently to earth, I ran into the kitchen and invited my mother to come and watch the next performance. But, naturally, once I'd got her into position as an audience, I couldn't get airborne. I just lay on the hearth rug, turning purple with effort, until she went angrily back to peeling her potatoes.

Perhaps it was all a dream or an elaborate game. I really don't know. It certainly created a lot of trouble. My mother talked it over with my father. Tiptoeing down to the lavatory I loitered to eavesdrop at their bedroom door.

'It's something she's read,' said my father in the tone he used to blame the tinned salmon for upset stomachs.

Afterwards they both became rather stiff and watchful, developing a mood in which they were singularly unreceptive to badgers. In the 1940s badgers were quite rare in England. They appeared mostly in nature books or stories like *The Wind in the Willows*, and, although there was then quite a bit of genuine countryside left in the gaps between the southern cities, were very seldom seen in woods and fields. They are nocturnal animals, coloured silver-grey like the moonlit floor of a forest, with black stripes on their faces like the shadows of night-trees. In 1945, at the end of the Second World War, we moved out of Bristol into the Severn valley. I lived there for most of the next ten years and often went for long walks through copses, lanes and deserted uplands. But in all that time I never saw a badger and nor did anyone else that I ever heard of in those quiet, elm-embowered villages.

So it was, after all, rather surprising that, one afternoon in 1940, I should meet a badger walking along a street in the middle of Bristol. Every day I went home from school for lunch and every day at about a quarter to two I walked back up Carnavon and Limerick Roads to spend an hour and a half with reading books or raffia mats at the low, green, kindergarten tables.

The badger came down the middle of the road in a busy determined way. I knew at once what it was because I had seen pictures in *Country Rambles for Juniors* and *Woodland Folk*. From these same books I knew that badgers were very strong, had sharp teeth and were not to be trifled with. So I hid behind one of the plane trees that were planted at regular intervals up and down each side of Limerick Road. The badger faltered. Perhaps it caught my scent. It turned away, mounted the far pavement and moved slowly through a half-open garden gate. I crept out and followed it. Through the railing I could see it snuffling in some wallflowers. I thought of going up the garden path, edging silently past the badger, ringing the bell and saying to whoever might answer the door, 'Excuse me, please. There's a badger in your flowers.'

Perhaps, like my mother when I told her I could fly, this person would agree to check my story. Perhaps the badger would hear us coming, take fright and hide itself or run away. Perhaps then the person who lived in the house would get angry. I thought about all this. On the whole it seemed likely that the householder would react badly even before we went in search of the badger, that the very word would evoke indignant rage. It would, after all, take a special kind of person to believe that so rare and shy a creature had quit the wild and travelled for many miles on its stumpy legs to inspect a herbaceous border in Limerick Road. So, after a time, I went on my way to school.

All through that long afternoon I never said a word about the badger to Miss Northcote or Josephine or even my special friend, Jane Morgan. At home I sat by the fire with my head on my knees and thought about the badger waking up in its sett and saying to itself, 'Today I will go forth and seek my fortune.' I thought of Mrs Badger watching with wonder and fear as her son went trotting away in the morning mist, and Mr Badger saying glumly, 'It's something he's read.'

At last I could hold out no longer. I told them at suppertime over the liver and onions. My brother said 'Ha! Ha!' My parents looked severe and mouthed at each other. There was a heavy silence while they worked out how to deal with me. In the end they said, 'What about Matilda and the matches?'

They told me that Matilda was always telling lies, calling the fire brigade for nothing. Then, one day, when her house was really blazing, nobody would believe her shrieks of 'Fire!' and she was burnt to cinders. This gave me the idea that they had no faith in my badger. I started crying again, worked myself up into a state and soon had everyone talking so volubly about badgers that the word began to drift away from its meaning, to sound like the chattered title of a Turkish princeling: 'Baja! Baja! Baja!'

But the following evening when my father was reading the *Evening Post*, he came upon an item headed BADGER BAFFLES ZOO EXPERT. He read out to us all that yesterday a fully-grown male badger had appeared mysteriously in Limerick Road. It had entered the garden of number twenty-five and dug a hole some ten feet deep. The householders, like Matilda, had called the fire brigade, who managed to extricate the badger and take it to the zoo. There, it seemed, the badger expert was baffled. The nearest woods where any self-respecting badger might live were at least ten miles away, which seemed a considerable hike for an animal with such short legs. Perhaps it was a pet that had escaped. But nobody had reported losing a badger and, so far as I know, nobody ever appeared to lay claim to it.

When she heard all this, my mother, who was very honourable, apologised. But afterwards she kept looking at me oddly out of the corner of her eye, rather as though she expected at any moment that I might rise from the ground and float quietly up to the ceiling. When she got up to see if her fish pie was ready, she gave herself a covert glance in the mirror and smiled in a quick uncertain way, as though, for a giddy moment, she saw the face of a girl of twenty-one.

Enthusiastic discussion about puddings

Margaret was my honours supervisor in 1979. I remember on a couple of occasions heading off on a Saturday morning with a draft of my thesis under my arm and climbing those stairs through the garden to the Boddy-Scott household in Bathurst Street—the house was stately, rather boat-like in nautical blue and white then, as I recall—to ring the big brass doorbell. On each occasion, Michael Scott answered the door with a genteel welcome saying 'Margaret will be along soon'. He showed me into the study and offered a sherry which I'd accept, then leave me for a time to contemplate the books, the pictures, returning with a tumbler full. I'd take a sip and we'd start to talk.

Mostly he did the talking and I did the listening. He was a good storyteller. While I was listening, I wondered about the story behind the portrait near to which he sat, a small one, of him in a turban looking like Lawrence of Arabia. The likeness between the painting and the person was striking. I would listen and listen, and eventually, when the sherry was nearing the bottom of the glass, Margaret would appear. By then, all considerations of Emily Dickinson and Sylvia Plath had evaporated. I'd end up, after an enjoyable talk about something else, staggering home legless and make another time to discuss the thesis in the smoke-screened university office later in the week.

Margaret was generous to me with her time that year. Jennifer Livett has said that students loved her because of who she was. We were her fond audience long before she appeared on prime time television. As a lecturer, she had great presence, of course; she was thoroughly engaging. But in those early years of my beginning to write and publish poetry, I was and still am grateful for the time Margaret took at an intensely busy period in her life, to write—in that characteristic handwriting—lengthy and detailed critical responses to some of my early poems.

Probably the period in which I saw Margaret the most, was in the late eighties, when she and Stephen Edgar and Andrew Sant and myself held dinner parties, during which a topic would present itself as the basis of poems we would then go away and write. The first was the Hobart snowfall of 1986, the second was phobias, and then country houses and other subjects followed. The revelation of what we had each produced before we met again was always exciting—four entirely different poetic responses. There was a lot of laughter on those evenings, and some enthusiastic discussion about puddings.

Sarah Day
Poet

Rollo, my hero

At twelve I took up the passion of my peers. I fell in love with the horse. This, if you wanted more than a short flirtation, was a demanding business. There was the theory, which involved learning a language full of words like 'crupper' and 'martingale' along with the special dialects of the hunting field and showground. And there was the practice, which meant nagging your parents into paying for riding lessons, mastering the art of rising at the trot, and then setting your sights on owning a pony who would carry you onward and upward to all kinds of astonishing adventures and triumph in the ring at White City.

The theory could be learned from two kinds of books. There were the manuals—*My First Pony*, *Riding For Beginners*—which had lots of pictures of horses, saddles, bridles and other equipment (called 'tack'). The horses in these books were stuck full of arrowlike black lines with little labels attached to the blunt ends: hoof, coronet, frog, pastern, cannon-bone… they made exhausting reading. But then there were the pony books, romances about horses and young girls, which set out to make all the lore more palatable. ('I say,' called Bunty, 'pass the dandy brush, Collie. Rollo's withers are simply caked with mud.')

As well as teaching you about withers and dandy brushes, *A Pony For Bunty* or *Rollo Wins Through* were fairly strong on social attitudes. I quickly learned that it was only the fat daughters of the nouveaux riches who rode to hounds on ponies they couldn't manage and talked about red coats instead of pink ones. Sometimes these horrid girls, who had vulgar accents and names like Edwina Mumps, committed a still more heinous social sin by referring to the baying pack that pursued the fox as 'the hounds' instead of 'hounds'. Despite this, the heroines—Bunty Truman, Collie Armstrong, et al—always rode gallantly to rescue the dreadful Edwinas when their ill-mannered, overbred ponies ran away with them and went speeding with suicidal purpose towards precipices, quicksands and express trains.

Girls like Bunty and Collie had parents who were TD ('topdrawer') but down on their luck. Their fathers were former air aces who limped, or mountaineers who had been detained in the Himalayas. Their mothers often kept guesthouses or riding schools and always had tired blue eyes. Late at night, weary with poring over her accounts, Bunty's mother would draw a thin hand across those tired eyes and sigh, 'I'm such a duffer at figures, darling!'

Lack of the readies meant that Bunty's and Collie's mounts were small and hairy. But behind these ponies' shaggy, tumbling forelocks gleamed eyes that were never the very least bit tired. They positively glowed, in fact, at all times with awesome superhuman intelligence. It was mere child's play for an animal like Bunty's Rollo to calculate, as he rushed to Edwina's rescue, the exact speed and angle of approach required to head off the runaways on the extreme edge of the cliff or the lip of the treacherous morass. The 11.45, thundering down from London, brought another factor into Rollo's calculations but nothing daunted him. He never failed to halt

Edwina just as she reached the top of the embankment at the very moment the train went roaring by.

After the rescue, Rollo would always stand patiently while the master of hounds came dashing up in his pink (ie red) coat, shouting, 'Bravo Bunty! My word, what a plucky pair!' And Julia Locksley-Bannerman, smiling down from her champion showjumper, would ask Bunty up to the Hall for a round of jumps with, possibly, a spot of muffin to follow. Then, at about this point, Mr and Mrs Mumps would appear, quivering like fat white jellies and sobbing thanks in common broken accents. Mr Mumps would bring out his chequebook and present Bunty with a token of appreciation large enough to put Bunty's mother's business back on its legs, after which everything was bound to go on splendidly, provided, of course, that Bunty's mother gave up messing about with the accounts and left them all to Rollo.

My own pony, when I finally acquired one, was not quite in Rollo's class. In fact, as a first pony for a child with no more practical knowledge of horses than the Mumps family, she was very nearly the worst possible choice. Young, strong, flighty and very badly schooled, she had a mouth like iron and a habit of treating any sort of jump like one of the banks or mounds she had met in her native Ireland. This meant, instead of jumping over rails, gates and white-painted oil drums, she jumped heavily and deliberately on top of them.

The trouble began almost immediately. There was a wonderful minute when we cantered up the grassy hill behind Kilkenny's paddock and entered Macey's Wood. The trees were in new leaf, the ground a carpet of bluebells and dappled sunshine. Life became, for a single shining moment, the stuff of dreams, then someone hunting rabbits deep in the wood fired a shotgun and Kilkenny bolted. She did this dozens of times during the next two or three years. After a few months I got quite used to it, but that first time was terrifying. Worse, it was dreadfully shaming. Fate, it seemed, had cast me as Edwina when, more than anything, I wanted to be Bunty. At least there was no precipice, no quagmire, no speeding train, nor, mercifully, was Bunty or anyone else there to see as I rushed wailing through the trees, reins and stirrups bouncing and flapping around me.

'Stop!' I sobbed. 'Stop! Please stop!'

Now Rollo, who never bolted anyway, would have responded at once to this plea from his young mistress but Kilkenny took no notice at all. She just galloped on until she got bored, then suddenly came to a halt and put down her head. I shot forward, landing heavily in some long grass which Kilkenny had already begun to munch. I clambered into the saddle again and tugged at the reins but she wouldn't stop eating whatever I did, so in the end I had to get off and drag her home on foot.

I tried to reason with her as we plodded along but it was no good. It was never any good, although for years I went on talking to her as though she had Rollo's mighty brain and, somewhere under her baffling perversity, his noble heart. In fact, as I began to realise when I was about fifteen, she was just an ordinary horse. She didn't even like me very much. When Bunty was in low spirits, Rollo nuzzled her cheek and, taking a fold of her hacking jacket gently in his teeth, led her off to look at some heartening discovery — Julia's lost diamond tiepin lying glinting in the hay or something like that. Kilkenny only nuzzled when she thought I might have an apple in my pocket and, if she couldn't get at it, put back her ears and bit right through my jodphurs into my leg.

Looking back, it seems odd I wouldn't give her up for a less troublesome pony. I kept thinking, I suppose, that soon Kilkenny would learn to love and obey, and everything would be all right. I could see so clearly how things ought to be—the Pony Club polocrosse matches in which she and I would lead our team to victory; the clear rounds in the children's showjumping classes; the fences gallantly cleared on the hunting field. As it was, even when Kilkenny decided not to flatten a fence, we very rarely went over it together. Usually she dug in her toes and I flew on alone. I had three broken fingers and a hairless patch where I'd cut my head diving onto a chain harrow. I used to limp home and creep up to my bedroom. There would be *Bunty Makes Good* and *Rollo to the Rescue* in their familiar places on the bookshelf, but I didn't feel like reading them anymore.

By now I'd begun to feel for Edwina. Like her, I'd acquired a nasty reputation for smashing jumps and disrupting Pony Club rallies. On one terrible occasion Kilkenny had actually floundered among hounds and trodden on a paw. After that I gave up hunting for months, but eventually, disguised in a new bowler hat, I ventured out to a meet at the local pub. Unfortunately, a bossy aunt who had come to stay with us decided to stroll down to watch the hunt move off. She must have heard about the hound-trampling incident because she hailed me from afar, warning me at the top of her voice to keep away from the dogs. I nearly died. Not only 'the' but 'dogs!' Even Edwina had never gone that far!

I sidled up to her and muttered, 'They're not dogs.'

Aunt May looked closely at the brown and white animals milling round the master's horse. She looked carefully at me.

'Over there,' she said. 'With the man in the red coat.'

'Pink, pink!' I hissed. 'It's a pink coat!'

That shut her up.

After a time, of course, Kilkenny got older and steadier while I got stronger and more experienced. Things started to look up. One day a man called Mitchell asked me to ride his horse in a point-to-point, though I think he was drunk at the time. It never came to anything because Mitchell died of a heart attack weeks before the race, probably when he sobered up enough to realise what he'd done. I never got to be the rider Bunty was any more than Kilkenny ever became a prodigy like Rollo. We never passed from hound-trampling to glory on the hunting field. In fact, we gave up hunting altogether quite soon after the meet Aunty May had watched. This was partly because the master, not misled for a minute by the bowler, continued frosty, but more because, as Edwina's stocks rose, Bunty's declined. I began to question Bunty's way of looking at things—foxes, for instance, and the poor old wobbling Mumpses.

My last year with Kilkenny was quite harmonious. I just stopped caring very much about what she felt for me, and, once I gave up acting as though we were married and treated her with detached commonsense, she became quite meek. Perhaps, with one single gleam of Rollo-like intelligence, she discerned that by now I had other fish to fry and she, at last, had been let off the hook.

Henceforward neither she nor any other horse would be expected to carry the dreams of which fiction is made into my life. My reading was changing. I'd discovered Byron, Georgette Heyer and *Wuthering Heights*. The vicar's son, a mild-mannered lad who played the bassoon, had invited me to go with him to the pictures. Poor youth! He never understood my smouldering glances. How could he know any more than Kilkenny the role he was meant to play? In any case, he'd never have had the nerve to rouse the vicarage by flinging open his window and shrieking my name to the storm. I persevered with him for a while then left him to cast about for more promising material. It was a surprisingly long time before I could accept that Heathcliff, like Rollo, had never had a counterpart in this humdrum world.

An ancient time glows in the memory

I first met Margaret Scott in 1960, in the Elbow Room of the New Sydney Hotel in Bathurst Street, opposite the Playhouse. She and her then husband, Michael Boddy, newly arrived from England, had joined our regular Friday night crowd for drinks.

That is an ancient time, and the Elbow Room, which no longer exists, glows in the memory, as do the cast of characters who gathered there: notably Peter Thompson and his wife Peggy, the painter Alan Frost, ABC drama producer John Baldwin, and local actors such as Mark Lyons-Reid. The pub was run by Roger Triffit (like his brother, a man of the theatre), and he'd styled the Elbow Room to be a sort of greenroom for the Playhouse. Softly lit, tastefully furnished, with Toulouse Lautrec prints on the walls and a wood-fire blazing on winter nights, it resembled a private club. Rough strangers, occasionally appearing at the door, were deceived into thinking that this was what it was, and would hastily retreat to the loud public bar across the hallway. Plump Bill the barman, with his Persil-white hair and jacket and his perfect manners, behaved exactly like a club steward. When he sold you a packet of cigarettes, he would slit it open and shake out the first cigarette. He also exerted firm control: Frostie was once banned for three weeks for walking on top of the bar.

The Elbow Room's regulars were the core of Hobart's artistic fraternity at that time; but that term doesn't really describe them. Mostly products of the 1930s and World War Two (Thompson, as a flight lieutenant in the RAF, had bombed Germany), they were rumbustious, old-style Bohemians, who refused to let middle age stop them being rumbustious—and their drinking was heroic. Starting in the Elbow Room, the evening would take us on to other pubs, and finally to somebody's home—usually Thompson's—where drinking would continue until the early hours of the morning. Thompson was always in charge of the evening, and it proceeded to a military schedule that he had laid down. ('It is now twenty-one hundred hours. We will proceed to the Sir William Don. You may smoke.')

This was the fraternity that Michael and Margaret Boddy joined, and they were welcomed with enthusiasm. Apart from their wit and good humour, we had gained in Boddy a wonderful folk singer: he would stand at the bar and give us such ballads as 'The Curragh of Kildare'—and I have never heard them sung better. Golden-haired and of enormous girth, he resembled a young Friar Tuck; he was teaching at the Hobart High School, and fame and fortune in the theatre on the mainland still lay ahead of him. As for Margaret, I remember her as self-contained, rather quiet, and somewhat obscured by Michael's mighty shadow. She was remarkably obliging, as well. One night, we all descended on the Boddy home after the pubs shut: a tall Victorian house in New Town Road. The mighty Boddy demanded food, lots of food, and I can still see Margaret hurrying about with the sorts of steaming dishes that would have satisfied Friar Tuck.

None of us had any idea then that she wrote poetry. Perhaps she didn't, at that stage. I left Tasmania soon afterwards and, except for a brief period in 1966, when she and her second husband Michael Scott were to be found in the Elbow Room,

I seldom encountered her again—except on the television screen. But of course, I discovered her poetry.

I did so with profound surprise, not having known that she was a poet. I put it in this way deliberately. In this period when schoolchildren are being encouraged to believe that their dismembered prose is poetry, we're being inundated with mountains of false verse—but true poets remain as rare as ever. The aphorism that they are born, not made, remains true; and Margaret Scott is the real thing. Her verse gives the sort of attention to form and metre that is technically beyond the reach of most amateurs now practising the craft, and consequently sings and echoes in the mind. But much more important than her technique is the authority of her emotional range, and her ability to bring off the great double theme of poetry: what the Welsh poet Alun Lewis called 'the single poetic theme of Life and Death … the question of what survives of the beloved'.

Added to this is her particular gift for dealing with the natural world. In this, to my mind, she bears comparison with the great Colette: in particular the Colette of *Sido*, that wonderful portrait of Colette's mother—a woman who was attuned to every flower in the garden and every wind that blew, and who could grow so excited by the beauty of a blackbird that she would not stop it eating her cherries. Very few poets could write unsentimentally of the death of a pet dog in a way that stabs at the heart, as Margaret Scott does in 'Prince'. Very few could write of cooking cabbage and potatoes and weave an alchemy whereby this humble domestic activity conjures up themes far beyond the kitchen. Like Colette, she can contemplate flowers and grass and all the fruits of the earth with a particular, intimate intensity which is perhaps uniquely feminine.

Margaret Scott is clearly one of Australia's foremost poets; and like all poets who deal naturally with universal themes, she does so through being attached to a region: in her case, her adopted home in Tasmania. In her exploration of this island's landscapes and its ghosts, she has come to rank in my mind with Gwen Harwood and Vivian Smith. But her vision is of course her own, often throwing a startling light on familiar scenes. And that, of course, is the ultimate gift of art.

Christopher Koch
Writer

In the shadows

Anyone walking that evening among the furze bushes of Hampstead Heath and pausing to gaze in the direction of the village might have been puzzled to observe a long snaking mass of lights jigging steadily along the London road. At times the stream poured in an unbroken flow, like a great sequined serpent, down the face of a distant hill; at others it broke into fragments as part of its length disappeared from view in some hidden valley, but always it came on, growing steadily in size. Slowly each point of light seemed to move apart from its fellows and to wag of its own volition, to smoke and flare, revealing among the hurrying throng of torches a huge shadowy mass of closely packed forms. Here and there the light caught the glint of harness as a cart or chaise pressed forward among the flood of running men, and soon the tramp of hurried footsteps on the freezing earth mingled with a furious murmur of voices.

The cavalcade erupted into the road that ran by the heath with a great roar of sound. By now, several lighter vehicles were jostling their way to the front of the column. The leaders whipped up their horses and went charging on with a thunder of hooves and whirling wheels, while the crowd broke open before them, yelling wildly.

The gates of the gloomy hospital were locked fast and supported by a great heap of lumber piled across the drive. But Devine had completely failed in his attempts to muster a large force of defenders. All day he had sent men off in every direction to beg for reinforcements, but the state of affairs in London had meant that no one could be spared. His messengers had returned alone or, often, had failed to return at all. He was left with some twenty men from his own division or from the local force, together with Richard Bradbrook and Stephen Fellowes, James Hartshorne and Obadiah Smith, Inspector Williams, a handful of servants and the six Guards officers who had arrived providentially an hour or so earlier.

Recognising the impossibility of defending the ground with so small a number, Devine had pulled all his men back to hold the house. Martha Bateson, with her son, and Mrs Hartshorne's other patients had been placed in the care of Elizabeth Fellowes, who had conveyed the whole party to the safety of Miss Lever's house in Welsford Avenue. Mrs Hartshorne herself and Dolly Miller had refused to leave the hospital and now sat among the defenders, silently awaiting the onslaught of the mob.

They heard the confused roar that arose when the torrent of men and vehicles fell like a wave upon the locked gates. Then came a great crashing and clanging as a dray, freed of its horses, was turned about, and with a score of people gripping the empty shafts and low sides, thrust like a battering ram against the rusty iron.

Meanwhile hundreds flowed away to each side, scrabbling up onto carts, shoulders and carriage roofs to scale the high walls. Men dropped in a black hail among the shrubs and withered garden plants, then ran to clear the blocked gateway so that within minutes the barricade in the drive was torn down. Then the chains on the gates burst and a mass of struggling horses and jolting vehicles poured in around the dray.

The heavy evergreens of the garden flashed into hectic colour as a river of lights went leaping and jogging its way beneath the trees. But for a moment, while the middle ranks of the column rushed forward, and the last of the rearguard came whooping and rattling over the heath, the leaders fell silent, baffled and cowed by the vast bulk of the castle-like mansion arising before them, by the total absence of any form of life and by the chill, dreary aspect of the place to which their final, frenzied, headlong rush had brought them. Then an upper window was thrown open and Superintendent Devine began in a clear, high voice to read the Riot Act. This had the effect of a spark dropped in dynamite. The crowd roared and surged forward, brandishing a forest of weapons. Some flung themselves at the heavy double doors that led into the hall, while others began to beat and hack at the windows, sending showers of broken glass flying among the besiegers.

Family album

Just before she died in the autumn of 1948, Grandma Duke gave Louie a photograph. It was the one she had kept by her bed in Howard Road among the medicine bottles and crumpled paper bags of liquorice allsorts. It had been taken, she told Louie, just after James first came down to Bristol. He was wearing a sailor suit and standing alone by a small table. His face looked soft and meek.

'I'd like you to have it, dear,' said old Liza-Jane.

The photograph was standing on her glass-topped hospital cupboard when Louie called in one day with a bag of grapes and a parcel of clean nightdresses. Louie stroked the purple velvet frame. Like Grandma Duke and everything else she owned, the lush material smelled faintly of worn coppers. The old woman lay among her pillows, slowly unwrapping her parcel with hands so fat and white they looked as though they were moulded out of lard.

'Did your mother iron these?' she asked, smoothing a crease. 'Dear, dear!'

Louie was taken aback at being given something that Grandma Duke prized so much. She knew very well that old Liza-Jane disliked her. She disliked all women and girls apart from humble, stringy creatures like Miss Wesley who put themselves at her service and listened in respectful amazement to tales of her affluent childhood and all that she'd thrown away when she married Bert. The only people that she seemed to like were big, jolly, handsome men, well-heeled, well set up, who chaffed her and winked and threw back their heads in echoing bellows of laughter. And, although he was nothing like that, she doted on James, or at least—so Louie thought—wanted more than anything else to have him dote on her and her alone. But she'd never bothered to lay out baits for his daughters. 'A real little madam,' she called Louie, complaining to James when he helped her up the stairs.

Watching Grandma Duke smiling bitterly at Beatrice's ironing, Louie realised that the photograph was not like other presents. It wasn't meant to give pleasure. All the old woman wanted was to vex Beatrice who had coveted the photograph for years and, now that Grandma Duke was dying, was expecting to claim it for herself.

Louie looked down at the floor. Old Liza-Jane gave an elaborate sigh, bundled up the nightdresses and pushed them away.

'If you've nothing to say to me, dear, you might as well go,' she said. 'You've got lots of better things to do than bothering about what I've got to put up with.'

So after a few minutes Louie went home and stood in the kitchen watching her mother who was kneeling on a mass of damp newspapers, scrubbing out the oven. She put the photograph on the table and said, 'Old Liza-Jane asked me to give you this.'

Beatrice squirmed round to look at what Louie had brought her.

'What?' she said. 'Never in the world! She gave it to you, didn't she?'

'I don't want it. You have it.'

'No, no. You keep it. But it was good of you to think of me like that.'

She smiled at Louie, pleased at being released into generosity. She had always thought of herself as open-handed, large-hearted, fond of parties and games, jokes and dancing. Often, over the years, she had nearly wept to think how the glowering presence upstairs, crouched in curtained gloom plotting against her butter, was crushing her down into an alien shape, squeezing out of her spirit drops of obsessive malice like unholy oil.

But, as the doctor had predicted, within less than a month, Beatrice was free of her enemy. On the day after Grandma Duke's death she went through the upstairs flat like a marauding army, throwing heaps of embroidered linen onto the floor, upending drawers full of letters, snapshots and liquorice. She found a Sunday school prize awarded to James Edward Phillips in 1898, several regimental photographs, a letter that James had written to the Dukes from Mesopotamia. In a trunk in the attic, under a pile of cases filled with the butterflies poor old Bert Duke had collected she found neatly tied bundles of receipts from customers whose clocks he and James had attended. At the bottom of the trunk there were more bundles made up of letters from Beatrice's father, Howard Gale, who had acted as the Dukes' solicitor. And another photograph showing young James standing with Bert Duke and a plump dark man with a fierce moustache, all holding butterfly nets. Behind them rose the ivied wall of what looked to be a very grand house. But there was nothing that shed any light on James's parentage or early life. It was not until the day of his funeral, thirty-eight years later, that the truth began to emerge.

Settling this corner of Tasmania

In *Changing Countries,* Margaret Scott recounts what seems to be her first child-hood memory. It is of crawling at night along an icy corridor to her parents' bedroom, to give them what she thought would be 'a marvelous surprise'. 'What's the trouble?' asks her father, the surprise 'falling rather flat' as the little one crawls into the warm bed and shocks her parents with her freezing feet. It strikes me as significant that Margaret's first memory is of wanting to give a surprise. I have memories of the time she and I spent in the English Department at the University of Tasmania that involve corridors and surprises.

One of the great joys of those years was Margaret appearing somewhat shyly at my door (she was at the other end of the corridor and this was in the days when colleagues still visited each other instead of emailing!) with a page in her hand, saying 'I've written a new poem. Would you like to see it?' She is very good at gifts of all kinds. I still enjoy the beautiful painted tray that she and her daughter Sarah brought me one Christmas—the day they returned home to the unpleasant surprise of having been burgled and had other gifts made off with. And I'm sitting looking at a cumquat tree that arrived literally out of the blue one day (we're now separated by considerable distance).

C S Lewis knew, though, what surprise really meant when he called his auto-biography *Surprised by Joy.* Surprise, like many (most) simple things has profound depths if we wish to seek them. Surprise is a reminder, potentially both joyful and chastening, at times frightening, that we are alive. Surprise as it recurs in many guises (often dark) in Margaret's experience and in her writing reflects a capacity for wonder and goodwill. It is deeply embedded in the poet's ability to make us see through fresh eyes the things of this world. 'A marvelous surprise' is what Margaret finds in the world and gives back to the world through her writing. It is the ca-pacity that enables both wonder and generosity to remain in the face of darkness. This capacity can be witnessed in the elegies on the death of her husband Michael Scott—an exceptionally fine set of poems that grew out of grief—and in Margaret's personal and written responses to the Port Arthur massacre in 1996.

Surprise helped to make Margaret a great teacher, beloved of her students. Deeply at home with an audience (ah, was that what the little girl creeping along the dark corridor was seeking?), Margaret was a superb lecturer, a gift that she continues to employ as a popular after-dinner speaker. What made her lectures and speeches so compelling? Well, for one thing, they were always rich in substance. Margaret plays a straight bat to our capacity for and love of good plain old facts (something that theories of education for some time have sought to deny). But the real trick is an unerring instinct for narrative—for storytelling. And surprise is story's basic ingredient: what in the world will happen next. Like great intellectual historians such as Frances Yates and Perry Miller, she knows that story + fact = idea. In other words, that ideas emerge out of the links we make among the things that constitute our world. Story adds to this process a relationship between teller and listener or writer and reader—a technique that involves the recipient. As listener or audience, we enjoy both anticipating and having things revealed to us—rather in the way that we enjoy the beautifully wrapped gift. The motivation for Margaret's novels, *The Baby Farmer* and *Family Album*, is not too far removed from that of her teaching. She begins with facts (respectively, the phenomenon of baby farming in the nineteenth century and a story from her own family); she delves into social history; she finds a compelling story to make sense of it all. And she revels in the surprises, the sometimes wily tricks, she will play on us, the readers.

Margaret's life has involved, a good deal more so than for many of us, the necessary or sometimes actively sought experience of the new: going to the new world of Cambridge University, daunting to a girl from Bristol; setting out for the new world of Australia to live and work, married and with a child, in her twenties; fires destroying two of her houses; taking early retirement to find a new life of writing, speaking engagements and lovingly working on old and new houses; and, perhaps above all, finding a new community on the Tasman Peninsula. Her own experiences of dislocation and starting afresh are reflected in a sensitivity to such experiences on the part of others. As I read through the poems recently, I was struck by the number that deal with not only personal migration but the larger story of settling this corner of Australia. The link, made so strongly in 'Return to Pirates Bay: Tasmania 1974', is almost an injunction for settlers old and new not to take this place for granted—to be prepared, as Margaret put it in a piece on the experience of exile, to become, and to remain, in the sense that it is all that we can ever reasonably be in this world, explorers.

Ruth Blair
Author

Infinity in the palm of your hand

In the summer of 1961, when I had lived in Tasmania for about a year, I set out with my family to visit Port Arthur for the first time. We drove in our old brown Ford over a dirt road for what seemed like—and probably was—half the day. Eventually we arrived at the look-out point on the hill above Eaglehawk Neck and gazed out over Pirates Bay to the towering rock formations of the Tasman Peninsula's east coast. I have never seen a view more beautiful than this and, as we journeyed on beyond the isthmus at the foot of the hill, I became aware that I was in a special place, that this Peninsula, dangling from the south-east corner of Australia's smallest state, is one of the scenic wonders of the world.

In those days I was an even more dedicated romantic than I am now, so that when we came to Port Arthur and saw the ruins of the prison that the British had built, I was filled with horror. The place itself was so wild and free. The scenes of mountain, forest and ocean all around Port Arthur were of the kind Romantic poets had hailed as sublime. Here, if anywhere on earth, the spirit might 'converse with Nature in true sympathy' and look into the heart of things, rising, I thought, to mystical commune with the Infinite. It seemed, then, utterly blasphemous to have chosen this, of all places, to serve as a prison, a site of restriction and confinement.

Worst of all was the deaf and dumb cell—a black punishment hole with double doors in which it was impossible to hear any sound or see anything but darkness. This cell would have been repulsive anywhere, but at Port Arthur where, out in the air the senses could drink in such rare and astonishing natural beauty, the black hole appeared as the most perverse and outrageous of obscenities. I felt as though the people who had conceived and built it had spat in the face of God.

When I got home after that excursion I wrote a bad and bitter sonnet and vowed never to visit the Tasman Peninsula again. I kept the vow for eighteen years, then, in the late summer of 1979, a friend offered to lend my family a holiday house— a shack—at Taranna, a few kilometres beyond Eaglehawk Neck, on the Arthur Highway.

After a good deal of negotiation with the children, most of whom wanted to do something else, I ended up setting out for a week at Taranna with just one—our youngest daughter, Sarah, who at the time was six years old. Together we had a holiday which both of us still remember as a fabulous golden time, a sequence of days full of sunshine and joyful surprises.

The first of these was the shack itself. *The Oxford English Dictionary* defines a shack as—among other things—'a roughly built cabin or shanty of logs, mud etc'. This was much what we were expecting when we arrived in Taranna one evening late in January. Instead we found a well built cottage equipped with a sink, a good electric stove, comfortable beds and chairs, even a bathroom with a shower and a hot water cylinder.

From this base, Sarah and I set out to explore the parts of the Peninsula which most visitors to Port Arthur never see. We turned off the tourist road to discover wonderful beaches: Fortescue Bay where Sarah learned to swim in the lagoon; Shelley Beach near Koonya; Lime Bay on the Peninsula's north-west tip; Roaring Beach and Crescent Bay with their huge ramparts of sand dunes; the sweeping arc of glittering white at Slopen Main.

Even in places well away from Port Arthur there were plenty of relics of a grim past, remnants of the chain of probation stations set up around Norfolk Bay to house convict gangs engaged on government works after the system of assignment to settler-masters had been abandoned. There were houses which had served as the residences of officials or station hospitals; a cemetery on a lonely headland; the ruins of the coal-mining settlement at Plunkett Point where prisoners were held in underground cells in between their shifts in the mines' depths. Yet, this time I was struck not so much by the crassness of the regime that had turned this lovely place into a gaol as by the way the Peninsula was slowly healing itself. Salt in the clay used to make convict bricks, the teeth of the wind and the rain were gradually hollowing out the confining walls. The bush was swallowing lime kilns, quarries and graves, the sea had brought down the jetties where transported men had loaded timber and coal onto waiting ships. And there were new people here now—farmers, fishermen and flower children, shopkeepers, teachers, councillors, mechanics. All we spoke to were friendly and helpful. New generations, a new community.

Ever since that summer over twenty years ago I have thought of the Tasman Peninsula as a place of renewal. Whatever happens, whatever horrors may be enacted here, wounds, it seems, can gradually be healed. Like the view of the ocean that I see from the front windows of my house, the whole place changes from day to day. It remakes itself, constantly growing; constantly dynamic, an ever-present reminder of new possibilities. All this makes up the first and most important reason why I live here and why I find the Peninsula an ideal place in which to work as a writer.

As time went on after 1979, my satisfaction at the natural world's power to overlay the scars inflicted in the convict era began to give way to a recognition of the need to preserve evidence of what once happened both at Port Arthur, at the penitentiary for secondary offenders, and in the probation stations scattered around Norfolk Bay. 'Those who cannot remember the past,' wrote Santayana in *The Life of Reason*, 'are condemned to repeat it.' But, as I gradually discovered, the Peninsula's convict ruins are much more than part of a salutary warning against ideologies with a greater capacity to reappear amongst us than we care to acknowledge. They are part of a renewal achieved not by wiping out the past but by coming to terms with it.

I can, perhaps, best explain what I mean by telling two stories. The first is one that I have told elsewhere. When the prison at Port Arthur was closed in 1877 and land on the Peninsula was opened to settlers, some of the first to arrive were the descendants of former convicts. The six Greatbatch brothers, who set up a farm at Nubeena in the early 1880s, were the sons of a man who had served time at Port Arthur. Other descendants of Port Arthur inmates, like the Palmers and the Gathercoles, settled still closer to the abandoned gaol. You might have thought that they would have turned on the penitentiary, the Commandant's house and the Model Prison and torn them stone from stone. But that is not what happened.

It is true that the Historic Site today is much less crowded with buildings than the model of the convict township set up in the Site's Museum. Any remaining structure made of wood was swept away in the bushfires that devastated Port Arthur in the 1890s. But afterwards, instead of carrying on where the fires had left off, the people who had come to live in the area set about adapting the remains of the prison to their own purposes.

The Commandant's house and the Junior Medical Officer's residence became hotels. Shops and new houses sprang up. The Parsonage, damaged in the fires, was restored to serve as the post office, in what was fast becoming a bustling township known as Carnarvon. Most significantly, the citizens of Carnarvon carefully restored the Asylum, which had housed those driven mad by the silence of the Model Prison, and used it as a social centre. Here, under one roof, were the local school, one of the best dance floors in the state, and, ultimately, the Tasman Council Chambers. While all across Australia and especially in the former Van Diemen's Land a new generation was seeking ways of living with or living down 'the hated stain', the people of the Tasman Peninsula set up an extraordinary metaphor. They preserved the past to become the ground for social interaction and the management of their own destiny. They made the suffering and madness of an earlier time the site of their children's education and planted in it their hopes for the future.

The second story concerned with change which seeks to recognise the past and draw sustenance from it is a more personal one. In 1984 when my husband, Michael Scott, died at the age of fifty-six, I had to confront the fact that the latter part of my life was going to be very different from what I had expected. I decided to take early retirement from the University of Tasmania where I had been teaching since 1966, to become a full-time writer and to make my home on the Tasman Peninsula which, ever since the holiday with Sarah, I'd been visiting whenever I got a chance. It also seemed a good idea to find some new, absorbing interest, something to challenge my constant preoccupation with loss. Like renovating a house. So, the best course, I decided, was to search the Peninsula not for a desirable residence, but for a semi-ruin, work on the place for a while and then move in. Eventually I discovered Tara, a large, once beautiful Federation homestead built by an orchardist in the days when the Peninsula was fast becoming one of Tasmania's foremost fruit growing areas. By 1985 the orchard industry had virtually disappeared, swept away by the loss of its export market when Britain joined the EEC, and Tara for years had stood empty apart from an increasing population of possums, swallows and rats.

All the major surgery the house required was carried out by an excellent local builder who put on a new roof, ripped off fibro extensions added in the 1940s, rebuilt the back section and created an upstairs bedroom. With his help, I planned the operation and did a good deal of the cosmetic work—stripping joinery, painting, working out colour schemes, and assembling carpets, curtains, white goods, light fittings and all kinds of other accessories. I also started laying out the garden in the paddock of waist-high grass surrounding the house.

The necessary subdivision of the land turned out to be very thorny, so after fixing on Tara in 1985 I had to wait for nearly two years before I could actually buy it and get to work. I spent this time making endless plans and finding out all I could about the history of the house and its owners. As a result, when work finally began, I knew what parts of the building were original and felt that I understood something of the vision that had guided the people who had first created the house. I have tried to remain true to that vision while adapting the place to my own time and my own needs. The result is a house whose restoration encompasses the restoration of my own life, a place which holds its past and mine together in the present, the new synthesis we both share.

The story of Carnarvon and the story of Tara show the area and the house in which I live as places in which evidence of the past is preserved as part of a continually evolving experience. Even more importantly, they demonstrate—I hope—a recognition of the need to understand and accept our history, if growth and change are to be genuinely fruitful.

All this adds up to a second reason, or set of reasons, for finding the Tasman Peninsula a place which nourishes my writing. Since settling here I've written a great deal which is concerned directly with the Peninsula's past: articles; poems which are being gathered up to form a collection called *Renovations* in which Tara has become a central metaphor; sections of the book on the Port Arthur massacre of 1996; and a short story about the redoubtable Mrs Jenkins, wife of the man who built Tara and a 'home industrialist' who, according to a *Mercury* newspaper article of 1944, processed some 250 different types of food in her kitchen. More importantly, living in this place where the past is ever-present has deepened and strengthened my interest in writing about ways of coming to terms with the past in other, different contexts. It has led me into shifting perceptions of what is called fiction and what is called history.

Another remarkable feature of the Tasman Peninsula, apparent in both its landscape and its population, is the existence of startling contrasts. At Eaglehawk Neck, if you look to one side you see the thundering breakers of Pirates Bay, a vast expanse of ocean running south to the Pole, and the awesome Gothic shapes of towering cliffs and rocks. On the other side of the isthmus there is a quiet inlet with tree-fringed shores where small boats ride on their own reflections and waterfowl gather. As you go on to explore the Peninsula further you find an extraordinary diversity of climate, land formation and wildlife: wetlands, rain forest, windswept heath and mountain, fertile farms and acres of rolling dunes. And the people who live in this strangely varied place are equally diverse. There are families who have lived on the same property for six or seven generations alongside artists, retirees and alternative life-stylers from Sydney or Darwin, Paris or New York. There are arch conservatives and fiery radicals, atheists, Zen Buddhists and people who talk to dolphins; farmers who grow truffles, musicians, computer experts and fishermen.

The result is that the Peninsula feels like a microcosm of something much bigger. Certainly, when you look at the history of the place, before and after the convict years, you might think you were studying a miniature version of the Australian experience at large, reduced to sharp lines, primary colours and intense contrasts. For at least five thousand years before any white men came here, the Peninsula was home to the Pydareme, a branch of the powerful Oyster Bay tribe which inhabited the southern part of Tasmania's east coast. While terrible things were done to indigenous people all over the mainland continent, on the Peninsula—the place of clear extremes—the Pydareme were completely destroyed. There seem to have been no survivors at all amongst the Aboriginal people that George Augustus Robinson met on his wanderings—only stories of a group spoken of in the past tense. After the convict period, during which the Peninsula became the largest prison in Australia, came the time of free settlement, 'the age of axe and billycan' when more timber was milled at Taranna than at any other place in any state of Australia. Then came the growth of agriculture; the First World War—whose effects on this small community still show out starkly; the Depression; the Second World War; Britain's entry into the EEC; attempts to produce commodities other than fruit—notably chickens—which have given way to the 'get big or get out' syndrome; the growth of tourism, with Port Arthur becoming the country's premier tourist destination, and now all kinds of experiments like breeding quail or bottling octopus, a high rate of unemployment, loss of services and fears for the future.

To live here, then, doesn't feel like living in a peaceful backwater. Since April 1996, when Port Arthur became the site of the worst peacetime massacre by a lone gunman anywhere in the world, we can no longer see our home as a haven, affording escape from the violence of the cities. Even before that, it was clear that a writer had no need to leave this community to understand much more than a single place or a single group of individuals. If you look closely you can read a wider, deeper story which supplies a bottomless well of material and stands as an image of what can be implied in the particular. You have only to look at the landscape—middens left behind by the Pydareme, the forests which have grown up behind the axemen of a hundred years ago, the farms swallowed up by the bush, the paddocks that were once orchards, the new communes and caravan parks, the young people crowding on the bus to town, the old shuffling across the road to the post office.

It's all there—but this, I suppose, might be said of any place in which a writer has come to feel at home, the place in which he or she has come to be part of a changeful and abiding landscape.

For Margaret

It is the warmth; most often it's the warmth.
There is, of course, the very famous wit,
but that's the candles on the cake. The voice,
perhaps, the icing. I would be
pushing this analogy uphill
with a very sharp pencil if I said
it's the ingredients that provide the nourishment
and if I added that the whole was cooked
with love I'd sound like a cross between
the CWA and a dodgy self-help book.

But it is your warmth, Margaret, above all else
that's brought us here in tribute, and the love
that you have learned for this island of exile
is what we all have read between your lines.

'Love', you once wrote, 'transforms the data
of the self', yet you look just the same
as when we first met. Then, again, to my eyes
so do I, so I'm not the best witness.
Perhaps the good news is we all stay young.
The Good News Week, however's another matter,
as are false eyelashes, croquembouche,
cabbage smells, dusting and stripping paint from doors.

Grief, too, is part of the whole,
both personal and communal, and the strength
that courage and honesty in facing it can give,
not only to yourself but to a whole
peninsula, a whole island.

Tim Thorne
Poet

Botanical pioneers

Many of the gardens made and tended by women in Australia were nostalgic places filled with old-fashioned flowers grown from seeds brought from 'Home'. Yet, as well as being the custodians of these exiles' mementos, women also took on the role of explorers in the discovery, recording and cultivation of native plants. The ability to draw and paint flowers, and the assembly of albums full of pressed and dried specimens, which were considered part of any accomplished young lady's skills in Victorian Britain, took on fresh significance in the New World as important tools of botanical exploration. The realisation that one might be sketching what had never been sketched, or pressing what had never been pressed, gave these familiar activities an entirely new thrill, which could easily develop into an obsession. So Louisa Clifton, who had come with her parents and siblings to settle at Australind, north of Bunbury, wrote in her diary on 24 May, 1841 that she had determined to make botanical studies the 'object and pursuit' of her leisure hours (Frost, 1984), while Georgiana Molloy, weighed down by ill health and the hardships of the settler's life, took comfort in collecting the seeds of native plants, eventually establishing an invaluable record of her discoveries through her correspondence with Captain Mangles.

In Tasmania, Louisa Anne Meredith, as well as producing meticulously executed paintings and drawings of indigenous plants and describing them in her prose writing, became, through her poetry, a different kind of botanical pioneer. She is one of the first Australian poets to look at her surroundings with delighted attention, recording her observations with such precision that she manages to show us a 'feathery fern tree' as it is, without confounding it with a palm or lamenting that it's not a willow (Smith & Scott, 1985). In this she is a kind of progenitrix of Furphy's Mary O'Halloran, born in the country she loves, 'a very creature of the phenomena which had environed her own dawning intelligence ... a child of the wilderness, a dryad among her kindred trees'. Mary has 'noticed the dusky aspect of the ironwood: the volumed cumuli of rich olive-green, crowning the lordly currajong; the darker shade of the wilga's mossy foliage-cataract'. Inevitably, after *Such is Life* appeared in 1903, she emerged as the new spirit of the old land, 'the perfect Young Australian'.

While it's not easy to imagine Xenia Jenkins as a dryad who communed with trees, she and Mary O'Halloran have several features in common. Mrs Jenkins's way of life, like her metal garden and the landscape surrounding her house, represents a synthesis of the Old World with the New, while Mary is both a member of the ancient 'Brito-Irish race' and the embodiment of the new Australia. Moreover, both figures are associated in one way or another with Paradise. Mary, the promise of the young nation's Edenic future, is described in language reminiscent of Genesis, naming her trees in the way that Adam gives names to all the newly created beasts and birds. Mrs Jenkins's garden has been described by those who remember it as 'a little Paradise', a phrase that recurs over and again in the tributes paid to gardens made by Australian women, such as the one established by Jill Ker Conway's mother at Coorain.

John Mitchel, one of the Irish political prisoners transported to Tasmania in the 1840s, remarks in his *Jail Journal* that he is presently in 'a land where not only the native productions of the country, but the very features of nature herself, seem formed on a pattern the reverse of every model, form and law on which the structure of the rest of the globe is put together'. He might have added that, while in the Old World Woman was held responsible for Paradise lost, in the New World, as creator of the antipodean garden, she had become the means by which it could be regained.

Margaret Scott and *Island*

The Australian winter of 1979 gave birth to a forty-two page stapled magazine on cheap paper entitled *The Tasmanian Review*, the product of a modest bevy of writers and academics, one of whom was Margaret Scott, who also contributed a poem.

Margaret Scott and Tasmania's national literary journal have been close ever since. Her relationship with it (*The Tasmanian Review* became *Island Magazine* with issue 6, 1981, and *Island* with issue 43/44, 1990) is unbroken. In its first decade she had poems and reviews published in it. During its second decade an awful crisis engulfed *Island*, and it seemed doomed, but Margaret united with others to save the magazine, and she helped initiate the formation of a management committee, upon which she served in difficult times from 1994 to 1999. On top of that she provided financial assistance (as did many others) which saved it from going the way of the thylacine. And during the third decade of *Island* she has been justly acknowledged in its pages. Following are a selection of words by or about her published in the magazine over the past quarter of a century.

From a review of two very different collections of poetry (*Island Magazine* 8, November 1981):

> *Sometimes we get our mudcrab on a toothpick and sometimes we get it in whacking great meaty dollops.*

From a review of Gwen Harwood's *The Lion's Bride* (*Island Magazine* 12, September 1982):

> *But, above all, music … is used, as in earlier poems, as an image of union or of some calm, some vision beyond the painful and the absurd. Sometimes music, like the sea, is the starting point for a complex exploration through which recurrent images persist as a central strand in the whole spreading web of the poem.*

But in that review Margaret remained steely-eyed:

> *In a poem that purports to be much concerned with the flesh, the speaker is a disembodied, oracular wraith, [and] the whole thing becomes oddly unconvincing, distant and cerebral …*

And brilliant:

> *Everyone, it seems, was eager that Gwen Harwood should stop playing games with her masks and come clean; now that she has apparently done so, some readers may find the full frontal stare unexpectedly petrifying.*

From a Port Arthur feature (*Island* 67, Winter 1996):

> *Local residents whose forebears were convicts say very little but hint sometimes that this is because they feel that nobody would listen, that the district's major employer [Port Arthur Historic Site] is out of their hands. 'You wouldn't have ghost tours of Anzac Cove,' said one quite recently. Well, no. You wouldn't.*

From an interview feature, 'Does Tasmania Have a Future?' (*Island* 72/73, Spring/Summer 1997):

> *I think the economic rationalist who always poses as being practical, sensible, and puts a value on material things is really very stupid because what is left out is what matters, like human relationships and quality of life. Quality of life is not a*

kidney-shaped swimming pool …

Why one needs a top level of [University of Tasmania] administrators who seem to spend half their highly paid lives on the Midland Highway, I really don't know…

I'm reminded of having to fill in forms about research projects in the English Department. Obviously the forms were designed for subjects other than arts subjects, for science or economics. You had to keep sort of bending and distorting what you actually wanted to say in order to fill in the boxes …

From an interview (*Island* 80/81, Spring/Summer 1999-2000)

I just love setting off from here (Tasman Peninsula) in my little car at six o'clock in the morning with only the swans and the cows to say goodbye and in four hours I am in the middle of Sydney …

I was enjoying myself very much and then the publishers announced that although they liked the chapters I had sent them, they didn't want a sequel after all. I got very glum about that … I had a feeling I was on a downward slide and then everything changed in a quite extraordinary way …

At the moment (writing Family Album*) I have all these charts and tables and lists of dates and all these people everywhere and sometimes I write about them and forget that they are meant to be dead …*

David Owen

Writer

Royal, real and republic

The game seems to have originated in the cloisters of French monasteries, along with other rather surprisingly unmonastic benefits to humanity like Benedictine and Chartreuse. Originally it was played with the open hand instead of a racket and was known as *jeu de paume*, or palm-play. The sporting monks were soon spotted by various young French knights who took up the game with a will and began to spread it around Europe. There is a record of 'tenys'—a name taken from the server's call of *tenez*—being introduced to Florence in 1325 and by the late fourteenth century it was established in England, where, as in France, it became popular with the upper crust and royalty.

In 1516, for instance, there is a record of ' blue velvet' purchased to make a 'tennis-coat' for King Henry VIII, who later had what is now the oldest royal tennis court in the world built at Hampton Court Palace. James I in 1599 referred to the game in his writing, while his eldest son, Prince Henry, died from a chill thought to have been caused by getting overheated during a tennis match. So royal the game certainly was.

The game played by King or Prince Henry was pretty close to modern royal tennis. By the middle of the sixteenth century, at least, rackets were introduced 'woven with strings such as are found on the six-string lyre', though whether these strings were ever actually strummed, on or off the court, I can't say. Whatever the case, up until the 1870s royal tennis dominated tennisdom. Before that there are a few scattered references to 'field tennis' played in the open air in an unenclosed space, but royal tennis was real tennis without doubt.

Lawn tennis began to forge ahead only when western inventors realised what could be done with rubber. The hard ball of real royal tennis wouldn't bounce on grass, but the invention of a rubberised bouncing ball changed everything. 'It is melancholy,' lamented the *St James's Gazette* in 1888, 'to see a word which has held its own for centuries gradually losing its connotation. Such a word is "tennis", by which nine persons out of ten today would understand the game of recent invention played on an unconfined court.' There were other laments as well: 'As with horsy women,' complained *Blackwood's Magazine*, 'tennisy girls become intolerable nuisances to their neighbours.'

But nothing could halt the march of lawn tennis. It swept the world. It arrived in Tasmania where prosperous orchardists, who built the house in which I now live on the Tasman Peninsula, laid out a tennis court in their garden. When I first moved in, neighbours kept coming round and saying, 'Mrs Jenkins, you know, had this place immaculate'; and then they would look at the ropy stretch of grass on which we play croquet for idiots and say bitterly, 'She had a tennis court and everything.'

After centuries of domination, then, real royal tennis is now much less widely played or known than the Mrs Jenkins variety. Moreover, looking back, you can see that, even in its heyday, the sport has not always had an easy ride. It has, in fact, been repeatedly attacked for a whole clutch of fascinating reasons, and at some points has been declared illegal.

First, it has been condemned for promoting quarrels. Take the word 'bandy'. This is a slippery term, as I know all too well. When I first arrived in Tasmania I heard about the bandicoot and inquired what it was. A mischievous person reminded me that a coot is a small black waterbird like a moorhen. 'Well,' he said, 'in Tassie coots have bandy legs.' I actually believed this for some years. But to resume—to bandy appears to have come into English meaning 'to strike a ball to and fro in tennis' but soon took on a wider, darker sense: to contend, strive, fight. The tennis court, then, was seen as a hotbed of strife.

Conversely, tennis was condemned as a frivolous, unmanly pastime which distracted young men from serious military exercises. You may remember that Shakespeare showed young Prince Hal being idle and dissolute in the *Henry IV* play, and the Prince at one stage chatting about tennis in Mistress Quickly's pub. Later, of course, Hal turns over a new leaf, puts tennis behind him, and emerges in *Henry V* as the ideal warrior king. Which is why he is not at all pleased when the Dauphin, son of the King of France, sends him a gift of tennis balls. He sees the gift as a deadly insult, a suggestion that he is still the lightweight, frivolous young fellow he once was. And he scorns the insolent gift in a famous speech:

> When we have matched our rackets to these balls, We will in France, by God's grace, play a set Shall strike his father's crown into the hazard. Tell him he hath made a match with such a wrangler That all the courts of France will be disturbed With chases.

Which is probably the most extended set of puns on the terminology of royal or real tennis ever written, and led, of course, to Laurence Olivier doing a lot of galloping.

Another reason for looking rather darkly on tennis lay in the onlooker's feeling that it was all a very chancy business, that you could never tell where the ball would end up, that the tennis court represented an anarchic world ruled by cruel Fortune rather than one watched over by divine Providence. Perhaps there have been times when you have felt like this. Anyway, the playwright Cyril Tourneur wrote in a moment of passion:

> Drop out mine eye-balls and let envious fortune Play at tennis with 'em.

Still more alarmingly, tennis was, of course, a foreign game. It was associated with Italy where, during the Renaissance period, leading families like the Borgias were mixed up in some very nasty sex scandals and seemed to be always trying to poison each other. And it had come from France. The French, even before the recent scrimmage over sewage, have never been popular in Britain. There has always been a worry about what a nice young Englishman might pick up in Paris—at best a taste for silly fashions, at worst a dose of what was known rather unfairly as the French disease. So says Sir Thomas Lovell, in yet another Shakespeare play (*Henry VIII*):

*They must … leave those remnants Of fool and feather that they got in France …
renouncing clean The faith they have in tennis and tall stockings …*

There is, however, no doubt that the main reason for denunciation of real royal tennis is that it has been seen over the centuries as immensely, undeniably SEXY. The original French name—palm-play—told it all. The game became linked in the popular imagination with groping hands, furtive hands, hands pressed secretly together. So Rice in his *Invective Against the Vices* of 1579 condemns bowling, dicing, carding, tennising and such like deeds and acts of the flesh; while poets turn repeatedly to tennis-references in their love poetry. The Earl of Surrey, for instance, writes that his eyes are so dazzled by gleams of love that he has oft missed the ball. Something which, I hope, does not oft happen to you.

Tennis, of course, makes you hot, which meant, perhaps, stripping off your shirt, which could, in turn, lead to anything. In John Webster's marvellous play, *The White Devil*, Duke Brachiano admits to going to his mistress's house to shift his shirt when he retires from tennis—and everyone of course knows what that means.

And heat—especially hot hands, hot palms—was in the seventeenth century and long before linked with the heat of desire. Desdemona's hot moist hand feeds Othello's suspicion of her infidelity, and another of Shakespeare's jealous husbands mutters 'Too hot, too hot!' when he sees his wife 'paddling palms and pinching fingers' with his best friend. Admittedly, neither Othello nor Leontes says anything about tennis, since women, although they may have preoccupied the players, didn't actually appear on any kind of tennis court until the nineteenth century.

Now, of course, things are very different. Women are admitted to this excellent Club and make full use of its splendid facilities. They will next year feature prominently in the Olympics—though not, unfortunately, as real royal tennis players. Moreover, since the attempt to change our constitution so that Australia would become a republic has failed, it might have been expected that a woman—the Queen—would open the Olympics.

I shall say little about the republic—my third R—since we've probably all heard quite enough on the subject for the moment. I'd just like to leave you with a rather happy thought produced by H G Nelson, as a way of soothing disappointed Republicans while satisfying the most rampant of Monarchists. His idea was that John Howard, our Prime Minister, should open the games dressed as the Queen. If Mr H were then to engage in a few exhibition bouts of real royal tennis with Malcolm Turnbull, John Clark, and Bronwyn Bishop dressed as Henry VIII, the widespread popularity of this ancient sport would be assured and the 2000 Olympics etched forever in the national memory.

Peripatetic travels with Margaret

What can I possibly contribute to this tribute? Hasn't everything been said? What can I add to the legends swirling around the marvellous Margaret Scott?

So much of her extraordinary life is on the public record. But there may, perhaps, be a few scraps of her CV with which you're unfamiliar.

I first met Margaret on the Ballarat goldfields in the lull before the storm of the Eureka Stockade. Though Margaret was dancing up a storm of her own. Her stage name, at the time, was Ruby Glitters and, night after night, she'd dance naked on the tabletops for debauched audiences of drunken diggers—who'd fling nuggets at her feet and sprinkle her glistening torso with gold dust.

After the insurrection she disappeared for a while, only to re-emerge as a double agent in some theatre of European conflict. As I recall, her pseudonym then was Mata Hari. There was the inevitable kerfuffle and Mata/Margaret was going to be martyred by firing squad … but at the last minute she slipped off into the darkness to re-emerge as a famous aviatrix who, yet again, would mysteriously vanish…

Margaret bobbed up again in Britain in a ménage with Edward VIII and Mrs Simpson. Appalled by their politics, she resumed her peripatetic existence and was sighted, variously, in Moscow, Washington, Buenos Aires, Peking and Paris … and in that romantic city formed yet another ménage with a European Resistance leader and an American drunk. Their story, later lightly fictionalised, was filmed as *Casablanca*, with Ingrid Bergman playing Margaret—though those of us who know and love Scott regard the impersonation by the Swedish actress as pallid and unconvincing.

More recently there was the sex scandal that helped bring down John Gorton and, of course, her subsequent affair with the late Jim Cairns. And all the time, Margaret was tossing off impeccable works of literature that should have won the Booker, the Vogel, the Franklin and the Nobel prizes, had it not been for the vicious interventions by the CIA.

Now Margaret is gracing Tasmania with her energetic and enigmatic presence and one awaits her next adventure with a mixture of awe and trepidation. But I, for one, will always remember her for a special, very personal reason … our rapturously romantic weekend in Venice during Carnivale in the early 1950 …

Phillip Adams
Broadcaster, columnist

A story of strength and courage

In December 1855 a proclamation was approved, substituting the name 'Tasmania' for that of 'Van Diemen's Land'. This was a relief to colonists of the better sort who knew all too well that, as 'Van Diemen's Land', their home had become notorious throughout the British Empire. Now, after more than a century of quiet in which much of the world beyond the ambit of Tasmanian tourist promotion has forgotten both the old name and the new, the island has become notorious again. And, of course, not just any part of the island. The tragedy of 28 April, 1996 was played out at Port Arthur, the most widely known of Van Diemen's Land's penal settlements, the darkest stain on its feared and tarnished name.

Once the colony had been renamed, the attempt to purge the place of its past led on to other changes. On the Tasman Peninsula, the former probation stations of Wedge Bay, Cascades and Impression Bay became, in time, the free settlements of Nubeena, Koonya and Premaydena. But at Port Arthur, which was supposed to become known as Carnarvon, the power of the old name proved too strong. Once a byword for the darkest facets of life in the nineteenth century, it has acquired an even more sinister reputation in the last decade of the twentieth.

So far as I know, nothing quite like this has occurred before. None of the Australian mass murders of the past took place at sites with a well-attested history of exceptional violence, pain and misery. Neither San Ysidro, California, where James Huberty killed twenty-one victims in July 1984, nor the English town of Hungerford where Michael Ryan shot dead sixteen people in August 1987 are places where people gathered to contemplate a peculiarly dark passage in their nation's history.

On 28 April, 1996 at Port Arthur, the reality of an earlier spate of suffering and death flashed for a moment, as though lit by a bolt of lightning. Many of those who heard gunshots thought a re-enactment of past events was in progress. One witness inside the Broad Arrow Cafe imagined the people, falling and dying around him were playing out some drama involving convicts and musketry. Only when he saw a woman shot in the temple and blood spurt from her head did he realise that he was watching a murderer in action then and there.

Others experienced a less terrible sense of double vision but became aware of the shadow of earlier cruelties moving behind the horrors of that April Sunday. It was as though the ghost of the convict past, which seemed to have been confronted and made tame, had come back, unplacated, to demand that we take stock all over again.

One reaction to this was to turn quickly away, to persist in the familiar denial of the past which, in the days before convict ancestors became fashionable, led to the wholesale destruction of records, the ostracism of aged relatives and the rejigging of family histories. In the week following the massacre there was a lot of talk of Tasmania's 'loss of innocence' as though the 'holiday isle' of the tourist brochures had never been Van Diemen's Land at all. At this members of the Aboriginal community protested—as well they might—that the history of the island state was very far from innocent since it encompassed the destruction of their forebears. There had been other massacres, other women and children—members of the indigenous population—shot down by men with guns. And some commentators, at least, recognised that innocence had not been the most prominent characteristic of mid-nineteenth century Port Arthur. The journalist Lindsay Simpson, amongst others, engaged in some trenchant criticism of the way in which the convict past, even when not denied, is habitually sanitised and sweetened. She went on to insist that the horrific events of this past as well as those of the present should be treated with a veracity which 'shows respect for those who died'.

Finally, there were those who laid emphasis on the atrocities of the convict period only to engage in another form of denial. Van Diemen's Land had been a place of darkness. In the end Tasmania had turned out to be no better. Leo Schofield, writing in *The Sunday Age* on 5 May, 1996, described a bushwalk in Tasmania, insisting that, during the walk he had 'felt that at some turn in the track, or emerging from an ancient forest of myrtles, I might be confronted with some inconceivable evil'.

The implications of this kind of thing, that Tasmania is somehow possessed by unspeakable forces, transform the island state from a microcosm encapsulating the essence of the Australian experience to a repository for evil, deftly excised from the fabric of mainland society, and transported, like the convicts themselves, to a suitably remote outpost.

Panic makes for dramatic scenes on film and good newspaper copy. The human stampede in which the weak are pushed aside and trampled has become part of the folklore of disaster so that we tend to expect extreme danger to produce a wild, destructive rush, like the one that turned Boston's Cocoanut Grove Night Club fire into a major catastrophe, back in 1942. Yet there was no wild panic in the Broad Arrow. As Damian Bugg stated, 'many of the people who were in the cafe at the time and survived to talk about it, spoke of little other noise than gunshot … the oppressive noise of the rapid fire of this gun'.

Five people ended up jammed together by the locked door in the gift shop, but the panicky stampede for safety, the screaming and clawing and thrusting away of the helpless, simply did not happen. Perhaps things went on so fast that there was no time for panic to set in, and yet that explanation won't quite do. People did react to the danger. A number of people pushed someone else out of the way, but never, it seems, to try and save themselves; it was always in an attempt to save another's life. Perhaps such behaviour is instinctive. If so, one can only say that these people had managed to live their lives in a way that kept their best instincts in remarkably good condition. They were generous, loving and brave and although many of them died, they demonstrated that, when put to the ultimate test, altruism is alive and well in late twentieth-century Australia. For that, in a time when it often seems that selflessness is an outdated virtue, we owe them an immeasurable debt.

L ast night I sat with Naomi on my front verandah overlooking the glimmering expanse of Prices Bay. We agreed that behind all the recent troubles lies the central question of how we see the past and that there will never be lasting peace until we recognise the wrongs that have been done, the horrors that have been perpetrated, without pretence or exaggeration. We cannot pretend that the convict experience or the massacre never happened but neither can we see the men who created the convict system or Martin Bryant as so vile that they are no longer human beings.

Naomi said:

'We need to try to understand what made them like they were—or are. If we just push them away it might all happen again. We've got to have an honest relationship with the past or we'll never get our heads right, we'll never know who we are. And we'll never get the tourism thing right either because we won't have anything real to show the tourists. At least we've got to get them looking at real questions about how they see the convict—and how they see us, living here on the Peninsula.'

After Naomi had gone home I sat on for a long time in the darkness. I believe what she had said is quite true, but I wished that I had said to her that the inevitable accompaniment of honestly facing cruelty and pain is an equivalent recognition of compassion and courage. These qualities come often in such ordinary forms that you may not recognise them but they are there all the same: in the people of the Broad Arrow, in everyone who has worked and struggled to overcome the effects of the massacre, in the community where it occurred. Finally, I remembered some words spoken at a memorial service in Hobart on the Friday after the shooting.

We have choices between shutting doors and opening them, between withdrawal and advance. Some people have said recently that they will never eat in a restaurant again, never go for a Sunday drive … But there is, as it were, a flip side to this fear. Perhaps we do well to remember that we are never absolutely safe, that some freakish event might strike us down—or those we love—at any moment. But one outcome of that is to live each day as if it were our last and to value those who are dear to us more highly. Similarly we can turn away from the world, throw up barricades, try to keep out anything that smacks of violence. Or we can look now with new eyes at films of Bosnia and Rwanda, at families standing in rubble mourning their dead in the latest war zone. We can feel new sympathy, do more, because it is now apparent that we are not exempt, we are like them in more ways than we believed.

We live in a place of extraordinary beauty. The beaches, the rock formations, the forests are still there in the autumn sunlight as they were last Sunday, as they will be—one hopes and trusts—for generations to come. When we look at them if we can remember these thirty-five deaths in a way that makes us live more humanely, more intensely, with broader sympathy, then some good may be brought out of this evil. The victims will not have died in vain and we will raise for them a memorial more fitting than anything wrought in stone.

Late and Soon
for Margaret Scott

A way of seeing divides choice and fate.
What we desire we may desire too soon.
Since time can't end, no moment is too late,

And like the rain each moment can but wait
To fall and where it falls is opportune.
A way of seeing divides choice and fate.

The sun is offered on the silver plate
It lays for you across the bay of noon.
Since time can't end, no moment is too late

And rising night may transubstantiate
That platter to the pale gold of the moon.
A way of seeing divides choice and fate,

As you have seen. A loss that might negate
Some lives you have transmuted to a boon.
Since time can't end, no moment is too late

To live as though each day has the same date,
As in utopia—or a cartoon.
A way of seeing divides choice and fate.
Since time can't end. No moment is too late.

Stephen Edgar
Poet

a little more

Selected Essays

Salvaging Tara

'I wish,' said my friend Val, 'that somebody could save Tara.' I put down my coffee and pricked up my ears. Perhaps Tara would turn out to be what I was looking for.

A few months earlier, after the death of my husband, I had made three decisions about the future: first, that I should find a project that would keep me from brooding, something that would absorb any spare time and energy that I might have; second, that I should eventually take early retirement from my job and become what I had always hoped to be—a full-time writer; third, that I should one day sell my house in Hobart and move to the Tasman Peninsula.

When I looked at those three aims together, it became obvious that what I had to do was to scour the Peninsula not for a ready-made Shangri-la but for something which could be gradually moulded into the ideal writer's retreat. The building or restoration of the house where I would one day live and work would become, then, the absorbing project that I needed.

I started driving about at weekends looking for 'For Sale' notices, struggling up tracks in the hills above Koonya, scrambling under barbed wire, staring disconsolately at lonely chimneys rising from clumps of brambles.

One Saturday I called on Val. Yes, she thought Tara might suit me very well. It was an old homestead on the Saltwater River Road, once very handsome but long derelict. The current owner, who had a quail farm, was planning to turn the house into a quail shed.

I drove to Price's Bay, stopped the car and gazed at the building on the rise to my left. It sat under the big Federation gable that framed its face like a battered sunbonnet, looking mutely at the sea with the air of someone who no longer cares about anything. There were bales of hay stacked on the verandah, strips of tape plastered over the cracked windows and a great staring blue rip on the eastern flank where somebody had started to dismantle a rickety extension.

Obviously, the house had come down a very long way in the world. It had once been, if not a stately home, at least a local showplace, standing in the midst of one of the flourishing orchard properties for which the Peninsula, like the Huon Valley, had been famous.

The orchardists who had built Tara had clearly decided to make a splash, to let themselves go and, in setting up their new home, to advertise their success. 'Mrs Jenkins,' I'd been told, 'had that place immaculate. She had a tennis court and everything.' But that had been almost seventy years ago. There was no sign of the tennis court when I was eventually allowed to inspect the house at close quarters.

An electric fence hemmed in a half-acre of shaggy grass. Cattle grazed on the level area beyond the fence where Mrs Jenkins' white-clad guests had once flitted to and fro in the shade of the clustering pine trees. You could almost hear their

voices still: 'Oh, Freddie, what a stunning service!'; 'Fault! Game to May and Frank!';
'Come on, Ethel, I'm dying for some lemonade!'

The inside of the house looked even sadder than the outside, neglected, battered and thick with dirt from the thousands of small flies that hung in clouds in every room. There were rats in the walls, possums in the chimneys and swallows nesting under the cornices. Worst of all, the decaying extensions on the east wall and at the back made the rooms of the original structure very dark. Tall windows that had looked out over orchards and tree-covered hills now offered a view of cobwebs and sagging fibro. Weatherboards had been stripped away and doorways cut in what had once been the outer walls.

All the same, I knew at once that this was the place for me. What magnetised me, I think, was that the designers of Tara had managed to combine the flamboyant with the practical and the conventional with the personal. The house faced north with shady verandahs at the front and on the western side. As in most Federation houses, the bay window jutting out at one end of the front verandah was topped by a high, steep gable. But Tara's gables looked to be a touch higher and steeper than most. At first this seemed to be no more than an exuberant flourish; very soon it became clear that the extra space in the roof helped to insulate the rooms beneath and the extra roof area meant that more rainwater was sent cascading into the household tank.

All the materials used in the original structure had been chosen to last. The stone for the foundations had been cut from the bluff on the eastern shore of Price's Bay, and lay, still covered in barnacles, as firm as on the day that it had been carted up by dray through the orchards. Virtually all the timber—including, as I was to discover, cedar, blackwood and flame Oregon—had stood up to years of weather, possums and itinerant apple pickers without flinching. Only the trim on the verandah posts, some doors and bits of joinery that had been smashed or wrenched down needed, in the end, to be replaced.

The builders who had put all this together—two English brothers called Barnicoat—had started work in 1915. Their price, according to local lore, amounted to one season's proceeds from the Jenkins's apples; for this they laboured through a full year to complete their commission: a homestead made up of a rectangular entrance hall with a reception room on either side and, beyond that, a passage with two bedrooms on the left and a kitchen, pantry and bathroom on the right. The back rooms were high, airy and plain, lined with Baltic pine. Elsewhere, some of the decoration, like the Art Nouveau arch separating drawing room and window bay, seemed entirely predictable, the sort of thing to be found in every Federation house from Burracoppin to Burradoo. Yet, whether because of the back-to-nature movement that began to influence home-building during World War I or because of their own sense of elegance, the designers of Tara had managed to avoid all the more folksy, fussy aspects of the Federation or Queen Anne style. They steered clear of inglenooks and mirror-panelled mantelpieces. Instead they added extra windows to the main rooms, decorated their fireplaces with beautifully carved gum leaves and blackwood pilasters, and, in the two front rooms and the hall, covered every available inch with an astonishing array of complementary designs in 'pressed tin'.

'Pressed tin'—which is, in fact, stamped zinc or steel—was all the rage in the earlier years of the century. The House of Wunderlich in Sydney produced cornices, panels and strips which could be tacked to a framework of battens, painted according to taste and, as the company advertisements pointed out, trusted to last a lifetime. Plaster ceilings were definitely out.

The Wunderlich copywriters cited instances of dinner parties disrupted by falling plaster, a Tamworth vicar bruised and shocked, a sideboard demolished. 'Banish this danger!' they urged. 'In place of dilapidation, Wunderlich brings the unfading charm of a patterned canopy, exquisite as some clean-chiselled bas-relief.' The builders of Tara were obviously impressed. They chose three patterned canopies with elaborate cornices, and then took the unusual step of adding Wunderlich wall panels. It could all have been rather overpowering but somebody—whether Mrs Jenkins or Mr Barnicoat—had a good eye.

They put Art Nouveau lilies on the walls of the larger reception room, a bold pattern of buds, leaves and tendrils in the smaller one and two samples of the handiwork of Samuel Rowe, Wunderlich's most noted designer, in the hall. It was the hall dado, made up of waratahs, stylised fruit trees and twirling ribands that won my heart the minute I set foot in the house.

Immediately, I began making plans. I wanted to restore the house to its original shape and elegance, but I didn't want a pantry full of meat hooks or a dunny in the garden. The extensions on the east side and at the back, which seemed to have been built in the early forties, would have to go, and the back one would have to be replaced by some carefully matched additions of my own. On the left there might be a side passage, a laundry, toilet and bathroom. On the right the original back wall, which was badly damaged, and the division between the old bathroom and pantry could be taken out, making space for a huge sociable kitchen of the kind I'd always wanted. Standing amidst the debris in a circling swarm of flies, I pictured groups of friends gathered about a wood stove and memorable meals cooked and carried through to the original kitchen, which was to be the dining room.

Although I was in a fever to get started, it was twenty months before all the details of the subdivision and sale could be completed. This was no bad thing because, while the outline of my first scheme for restoring Tara never altered, I changed my mind over details from one day to the next. It took a lot of visits to the derelict house, a lot of pacing, staring, measuring and researching before I could be reasonably sure of the most pleasing and practical way of doing things. Even then, of course, once work began we kept making discoveries that led to a string of minor modifications in the plans.

Before making a definite offer for Tara, I had asked a local builder, David Haywood, to look the place over. 'She's as sound as a drum,' he reported. 'But your biggest enemy's the roof.' He would take no payment for making the inspection but hoped that I would remember him when the time came to start work. Twenty months later I did remember him and found, very quickly, that David was the ideal man for the project. Patiently he redrew my plans for submission to the local Council. He then started clearing Tara of its resident wildlife. 'That possum,' he confided, 'came out of there like a bucket of boiling water.'

Once the necessary demolition was completed David set about replacing the old roof and framing up the new extension with all the conscientious craftsmanship of the original builders. He entered into the spirit of the thing, contributing ideas at every turn. Here was a line of windows with glazing bars. Might not the central window look better plain? He had an extraordinary fund of knowledge—not simply where to get skirting boards run off that would exactly match those in the existing passage but where to find old bricks or the right sort of wood stove. He happened to know of someone who wanted to sell a fireplace very like those already installed at Tara, and where to hire a floor sander at a good price.

All through the winter and spring of 1987, David worked away with his son. Every weekend I rushed down to see what progress had been made and was never disappointed. Every Sunday before driving back to Hobart I would leave more lists of instructions: Front room I: Replace glass in bay window and one side window; replace sash cords; remove built-in cupboard from alcove; repair panel (doorway to old extension) with spare pressed tin; repair door lock and put on door furniture; sand floor. All this the Haywoods would do, working, as time went on, alongside other tradesmen—the electrician who rewired the entire house and the plumber who was linking the huge brick water tank, built by the Jenkins family, to the taps in the new bathroom, kitchen and laundry. By Christmas 1987, Tara was, once again, habitable.

During all this first phase of the restoration my own part seemed to consist largely of shopping. The number of fixtures and fittings that needed to be chosen— not to mention paint, curtains, carpets and wallpaper for Phase Two—grew larger from day to day. I scoured Hobart for brass light switches, ceramic doorknobs, window catches, taps, tiles and slate for the new extension floor. I twiddled the knobs of a dozen cookers and washing machines, looked longingly at spas, frowned over wooden toilet seats, and chased up a pair of doors with cedar panels that had once hung in Hadley's Hotel.

Then there were craftspeople to be found: Karen Phillips—now my daughter-in-law—who made leadlight panels for the outer doors and a wonderful design of waratahs, complementing Samuel Rowe's pressed tin, for the panes around the door at the front of the house; Don Coomb, who made panelled celery top cupboards for the kitchen and bathroom; Peter Rigozzi who, amongst other things, helped me rescue the broken remnants of the verandah-post decorations from a patch of long grass, mended them and then made replacements, complete with turned knobs, for all those that were missing.

Once it was possible to stay at Tara it was time for the second phase of the project to begin. Work on various features of Phase One—some of them afterthoughts, like a bedroom in the roof—was still going on, but my own role was about to change from shopper to decorator. Early in the piece we had decided to take all the Baltic pine from the walls of the two original bedrooms and use it to line the new kitchen. The bedrooms, walled now with white plasterboard, stood stark and bare, awaiting a transforming touch. But before I could start painting and papering I had to strip the woodwork.

After scratching tentatively at a fireplace and finding that it was made of Huon pine and blackwood, I'd decided to strip all the joinery in the house, sand it and treat it with linseed oil or Estapol according to its position and the amount of wear and tear it would have to stand up to. There were times when I regretted this decision, not only because nobody could resist making jokes when I talked about all the stripping that I was doing, but also because stripping paint is a slow, dull, filthy job which does nasty things to your lungs, neck and arm muscles. And Tara has a great deal of joinery. Just for starters there are four external and eleven internal doors. Other items on the stripping list included nineteen architraves, two fireplaces, metres of cedar skirting board, twelve double-hung window frames, two ornate arches and the various panels and window frames surrounding both the front door and a second door that opens onto the verandah. Most of this was covered in several coats of cream paint, a coat of dark brown varnish and, in some cases, a fiendish blue kalsomine concoction that had soaked deep into the grain of the wood.

I tried every method of stripping known to man, ending up with a shelf of chemicals and a carton of implements. From time to time I weakened and sent a door off to be dipped in caustic soda, but even though I doused these doors in vinegar, sanded away and rubbed in pints of oil, they never quite regained the golden glow of the wood that was stripped by hand. In the end, then, it came down to simple hard yakka. Heat guns were not much use because they turned the layer of varnish to a clinging, spreading toffee; chemical strippers made the cedar black. After trying everything I came to rely most heavily on a razor-sharp scraper and fine steel wool soaked in turps. For mouldings and fiddly bits nothing could beat one half of a pair of broken nail scissors. I lived in terror lest somebody should throw this apparently worthless object away and took to hiding it under a brick on one of the chimneys.

Once the joinery in the first bedroom had been stripped I went out and bought some wallpaper. Then I chose curtain material, a carpet and doona covers to match. Having done this, I realised that a good way to proceed might be to choose some central item for each room, something that suited the house in a special way and appealed to me as particularly beautiful. After that I could build each colour-scheme around a centre core.

The big front room was fairly easy. I found a lovely William Morris print, a clear forerunner of Art Nouveau designs, which could be used to cover the two wing chairs I was planning to place on either side of the fireplace. Armed with a swatch of the material I set out for Tas Paints who mixed the exact shades of cream, gold, pink and green that were combined in the print. Various friends now turned up to help out. Dennis Tilyard scrubbed, primed and painted the pressed tin, Fay Aherne made loose covers, pelmets and curtains in William Morris greens. Always a glutton for punishment, I scrambled up a stepladder and began to pick out the flowers and leaves of the cornice in Tas Paints' carefully matched colours. By nightfall, I was complaining bitterly about my neck and hunting for Panadol.

In the dining room the core element was a Persian carpet from which I had to scratch microscopic samples of fluff.

The staff of Tas Paints remained quite calm, even though it can't be too easy to match a paint to a dot of cream or gold tucked away in the bottom of an envelope.

In the master bedroom the key to everything was a frieze from the Powerhouse Museum in Sydney. My son Daniel, who gave it to me as a Christmas present, realised that the waratah pattern was appropriate, but could not have known that Parnell Johnson, who designed the frieze, was a colleague of Samuel Rowe of Wunderlich or that the two shared an association with Lucien Henri, the artist credited with first introducing Australian flora into home decorating.

Discoveries like this lighted the way but the great discovery, revealed little by little, room by room, was the slowly emerging grace of the house itself. Gradually it blossomed and smiled, showing itself to have been even more beautiful than anyone could have suspected. Now that I live at Tara I often walk around, running a hand over an architrave, remembering the dust in summer, the draughts and bare boards in winter. I look out at the turquoise water of the bay or watch the sun going down behind the hill to the west. Then my eye falls on the patch where three truckloads of metal were dumped in the days when Tara was destined to become a quail shed. It took four years to restore the house. The garden may take a little longer.

A life rooted in the English language

I first heard of Margaret Scott in 1967, when Michael Boddy told me her house had burned down in the Hobart fires of that year. My house burned down in 1993 and her Premaydena farmhouse—one of the loveliest places I have ever visited—in 2003. So I can say with truth I know about half of how she felt, but not all; never all.

One responds to fire in a primal way. It seems to be a judgement. It negates you. It removes your photographs, your memories, your remaining sense of importance, your will to go on. This is not so with Margaret. She has been tried in the fire, as the saying goes, and has not been found wanting.

For what she has done in her life is rooted, I think, in something much less flammable: the English language. She daily climbs it like a child does an old loved tree. She knows its myriad branches and melodies by heart. In its writing she has what once was said of Robert Louis Stevenson, perfect pitch. Like Thoreau or Cardus or George Eliot she works the colloquial, and the common themes of humankind, into calm and lasting poetry.

Her books, however recent, seem to have been with us a long time; her poems likewise fixed and everlasting. Where this came from—and her infinite capacity to make deft luminous jokes—I can only guess at. It's possible some people are hooked into the race memory in a way that other people are not. It's possible some people are finer-tuned to the harmonies of sound and meaning that our sly language has hinted at from its beginnings, the extra shadings Tolkien found, and Keats, and Shakespeare, and Malory, in a syllable properly placed in a sequence.

It's possible this special faculty is the same one that also makes jokes, and gets a big laugh that is just one syllable distant from a small laugh or none at all. To hear Margaret in debate, and in the delicate shuttlecock of wit in contest, is to hear the language anew.

Margaret is an original, a rare sweet offshore island of thought, integrity and linguistic relish one visits with wonder, as one visits Tasmania itself. Like many great souls she thinks herself less grand than she should. She regards herself as a feature of the neighbourhood but not as what she is, the transformation of it. She is, I guess the Poet Laureate of Tasmania by acclamation already, and all who know her know it, but she herself is uncertain she has yet made the grade.

After evading as she inadvertently did all the glittering prizes of Oxbridge, the BBC and the dinner party set of Hampstead and Highgate, she may still feel there is a way to go to glory yet. She need not worry. Her glory is here, and now.

Bob Ellis
Writer

It's a jungle out there!

It took about four years to restore Tara, the once derelict Federation house on the Tasman Peninsula which is now my home. I moved in finally on 8 February, 1991 and spent the next two weeks arranging and rearranging furniture, ornaments and books. At last it was finished. I walked about proudly savouring the effect but found after a time that to achieve full satisfaction I needed to sit down. From a chair I could view the new paint, the carefully chosen fabrics and, beyond the windows, a vista of sky, trees and green hills dotted with sheep. When I stood up I was faced with the immediate foreground—approximately 7000 square metres of gently undulating, waist-high grass cured to the colour of straw—the garden.

I soon got rather touchy about it, hurrying visitors along the jungle paths to the house and saying airily, 'Of course I haven't done much outside yet, but I'm going to have a croquet lawn down there later on and I think a little orchard in that corner.'

Friends with no great interest in gardening usually laughed. The more knowledgeable looked from me to the nodding grasses and shook their heads.

'It won't be so hard,' I thought. 'Compared to the house the garden will be a pushover.'

But it wasn't. It was—and is—much harder.

This began to dawn on me one fine March morning when I sallied forth armed with a small pair of clippers. By lunchtime I felt like the girl in the fairy story who is locked up in a huge room full of straw and ordered to spin it all into gold by morning but I had at least begun to get some sense of the nature of the task before me and, more importantly, to appreciate the depths of my own ignorance.

That evening I pulled out the gardening books and started reading the chapters entitled 'Your New Garden' or 'Garden Design and Establishment'.

'Clear the ground,' they said, 'of rubbish.'

This wasn't very helpful. Any fool could have worked out I needed to get rid of the brick pallets and rusty paint tins that I'd been stumbling over all through the morning. The trouble was that until the grass had been slashed it was difficult to see the rubbish and even more difficult to haul it out, yet nobody could be expected to take a slasher through a wilderness full of booby traps.

'Sheep,' I thought. 'Possibly goats. There is no need to discriminate on this occasion.'

A kind neighbour brought along his flock. In they poured, 400 woolly whippersnippers ready for action. They had bad haircuts, long wrinkled necks and queer, light eyes with pupils like exclamation marks. Some of them were extremely spiteful and kept nipping their companions but this, I told myself, was of no consequence provided they also used their teeth on the grass. And they did. For two days and nights they trampled, tore and chewed until the whole block seemed strangely large, the trees looked taller and the ground rolled away littered with more derelict objects than are usually seen in photographs of the Somme. Next I borrowed a goat called Kelly who set to work on the blackberries. He did a remarkable job but was clever at unhooking his chain from its stake. When you are alone in a darkened house it is unnerving to be woken at dead of night by the sound of heavy footsteps on the veranda and the clanking chains. So Kelly went home again and I turned back to the gardening books.

'Make a plan,' they said. 'To be successful a planned approach is necessary.'

Some advised the use of overlays, others suggested coloured pencils for mapping out the herbaceous borders. That would be all very well, I thought later on. Meanwhile, after a few visits to the tip, I needed something basic, a rough sketch to help me identify the problems. Tentatively I drew a lopsided rectangle to represent the block which measures roughly 60 metres by 115, and lies at right angles to the track leading up from the sea. The entrance—two wooden gates—is in the middle of the boundary at the western end.

So far so good. Most of the perimeter was in excellent shape because David Haywood, the builder who had been working on the house, had erected a sturdy post and rail fence along nine-tenths of the boundary. There was only one section, extending from behind the house up into the south-west corner of the block, where the original dilapidated wire fence was still standing—or tottering. In one of the rare moments during the house restoration when I'd given a quick thought to the garden I'd noticed a windbreak was needed along that part of the boundary and I'd decided to plant many more trees and shrubs among the wattles and flowering gums already growing there.

'So why,' I'd asked myself, 'waste money on a new fence when it will be buried in shrubbery?'

'Because,' I might have answered myself had I been wiser, 'the young cattle in the paddock like poking their heads through the holes in the wire fence and one day they are going to pull it down.'

They are certainly trying. They keep the fence-line well grazed but that is no compensation for the pangs of terror that strike me when they yank their heads back and the whole fence twangs like a giant lyre.

Even in the days when I welcomed sheep I drew the line at cows.

Today, after hundreds of hours of digging and hacking, heaving rocks around and puffing up and down with barrows of soil, stones and manure, the thought of visiting cows makes my blood run cold.

But there is light on the horizon. I am planting wormwood all along the fence-line. It makes an attractive silvery hedge and cattle, although I've never noticed them riffling through a copy of Shakespeare, seem to know all about the bitter taste to which the bard refers in several plays. Having drawn the outline of the block I pencilled in all the permanent fixtures: the house which stands about a third of the way down the rectangle, with its west side opposite the entrance gates and its front veranda about 10 metres from the northern boundary; an L-shaped shed, part lock-up and part carport with trellised walls; two water tanks—one monster built of grey, homemade bricks which serves the house and one small, new tank for the garden, tucked away in the inner elbow of the shed; and trees—a huge, handsome gum and two pines at the eastern end of the block next to what had once been the original owners' tennis court; some younger gums and acacias running out from the south-west corner; a lovely robinia; some gnarled pittosporums and a few scattered cordylines, relics of the original garden, which, according to local legend, had once been a sight to behold.

One of the first questions to consider was the extent to which I should try to re-create this earlier garden. Rumours abounded. Someone remembered a laburnum tree, another remembered arum lilies. Everyone who was old enough remembered the tennis court. But nobody could produce a photograph or give any precise details of layout.

This wasn't altogether surprising because the original garden had obviously undergone some drastic changes even before the house had ceased to serve as the hub of a large orchard property. Extensions, which I had removed or replaced, had been added to the house in all directions. Fences and tracks had been moved hither and thither. There were cordylines and traces of stonework in several of the surrounding paddocks, suggesting that at one time the garden's shape had been quite different from that of the present block and much bigger. In recent years the area around the house had taken a terrible battering. Stock—including the helpful sheep—had trampled over it, tractors and builders' trucks had crunched up and down, two deep trenches had been dug for the electric cable and the telephone line and, worst of all, in the days when Tara had been scheduled to become a quail shed, three truckloads of smashed up road had been dumped in heaps between the gates and the house. Later, this devilish mixture of clay, chunks of bitumen and millions of small stones had been spread about half a metre deep all along the west side of the house and round to the back and front.

Despite all this I decided to engage in a bit of excavation and soon found that at one time the house had been surrounded by a wide bed edged with blocks of knobbly whitish cement. Outside this edging ran the remains of a path made of sandstone slabs.

Unearthing the bed and path became an obsession. I forgot to go to parties. My new novel hung fire. My friends who have been astonishingly patient and generous throughout the whole Tara exercise began to look a bit downcast. One, who was handed a pick the moment he got out of his car, complained that he felt like a victim of the Cultural Revolution. Others tried to turn the conversation to poetry, politics, the theatre but always I brought them back to mud and stones. I even bored taxi drivers with the story of how many centimetres I'd advanced since last week. Once, in Melbourne, I found a sympathetic ear. I was speeding towards Tullamarine in a taxi driven by a cheerful young man with a strong Greek accent.

'There is nothing I like better,' I told him, 'than to get outside with my pick and do a bit of digging.'

'In my village,' he said happily, 'we all have picks. In Greece everyone has picks for thousands of years. At Christmas we kill the pick and all the friends come in to eat it.'

It took a while to sort this out but we parted on good terms.

Meanwhile the plan and the planned approach had dropped into the background.

There were a few large features which had gradually become so firmly planted in my mind they seemed as immovable as the fixtures that already existed. One of these was the south-western shrubbery. Another was the croquet lawn. Since I've never been much good at tennis I had decided long before that the site of the tennis court ought to be used for croquet. I can't play croquet either but the idea of guests in white suits or filmy dresses and picture hats sipping fruit cup beneath the trees is very seductive.

So there was my sketch of the block dotted with fixtures present and to come and there it seemed to stick. I would draw in a path or a flowerbed and rub it out again.

'No,' I thought. 'I have to finish what I'm doing. I have to see the bed and the path round the house. Then I'll know what to do next.'

And so it has been ever since. Once a project has been more or less completed the next step has seemed inevitable. It may be that in working on one particular area I gradually come to know more about the patch next door—how exposed it is, what the soil and drainage are like, whether it affords a view that has to be preserved and, above all, how it might complement or flow into the section on which I am currently working. I'm not really sure why it is that decision after decision has seemed to make itself.

All I can say is that this domino technique suits me and seems to suit this particular site. It may not suit everyone and it has some obvious dangers. For instance, it is now impossible to take heavy machinery down to the old tennis court. The way is barred by a herb garden, shrubs and paths, so if we want to do any harrowing or anything of that kind before sowing the croquet lawn, the fence will have to be dismantled.

Once the bed around the house (well, on three sides anyway) had been disinterred and largely cleared of stones I began to learn a lot about soil. It seems amazing that if you keep on heaping up weeds on a barren patch you can actually create quite a good layer of topsoil. It also seems amazing that if you put a thick dressing of chicken manure on top of this soil then cover it with wet newspapers topped with hay you will have a bed in which most plants develop the lovely rich gloss of abundant health. There are practically no weeds either and you need to do little watering.

Some plants I was told prefer poor soil. This seemed an objectionable statement, like saying that the poor enjoy poverty and can't appreciate the pleasures of the rich. But it is true. Most Australian native plants hate chicken manure and many herbs, such as French tarragon, prefer a dryish, sandy soil to the dark, moist loam that it is such a pleasure to create. So I keep one of the beds in the herb garden free of compost, manure and all other enrichments, leaving the more determined ascetics to enjoy their dismal diet in peace.

The herb garden, like so much else, emerged as inevitable once the shape of the space it occupies had been determined by other developments. It has a large open centre paved with some of the stones which, once I began looking around, started popping up everywhere. There is a terracotta birdbath in the middle of the paved circle, standing in a little brick-edged bed of thyme and dianthus, and all around the circle there are large beds which are gradually filling up with various herbs, scented, culinary and medicinal. This part of the garden has become my pride and joy because it is here that some of the pleasures I've discovered in gardening are at their keenest.

One of these pleasures is catalogue reading. Rose catalogues are good partly because the names are nearly as sumptuous as the flowers: Kardinal, Pharaoh, Princese, La Stupenda, Lady X, Coral Sunset, Mexicana, Peer Gynt and Whisky Mac. But herb catalogues are better still, especially where some details of the plants' histories and traditional uses are given. There's meadowsweet, once strewn in churches at weddings, a great soother of nerves that, according to the seventeenth-century herbalist, Nicholas Culpeper, makes 'a merry heart'. Or lady's mantle *(Alchemilla vulgaris)* which takes its botanical name from alchemy because of its reputation for producing wonderful cures and restoring women's beauty. Or angelica, which even though it is used to flavour Chartreuse, French vermouths and anisette, is widely regarded as a cure for drunkenness.

Another enormous, composite pleasure of gardening in general and herb gardening in particular is that, although it can be a peacefully solitary occupation, it links the gardener with other human beings in the past, the present and the future. People have been making gardens for pleasure and spiritual refreshment for many thousands of years. King Sargon of Babylonia was importing roses from Cappadocia well before the writing of the Book of Genesis, and the Chinese appear to have been proficient at growing flowers and shrubs for centuries before that. Planting a yellow chrysanthemum or a peony becomes quite a solemn act when you reflect that Chinese gardeners were doing exactly the same thing when western Europe was still in the Stone Age.

The cultivation of herbs is even older than the making of pleasure gardens and, perhaps because of the secret, magical properties of many herbs, seems to create a kind of freemasonry between herb-growers of vastly different times and places. Reading that Pliny the Younger was having a spot of bother with his box hedges at his villa near Rome—the box withered where it was exposed to the sea wind and he had to replace it with rosemary—I nod sympathetically and think about dropping him a note ('Try wormwood!'). But, then, he died in about 113 AD.

Gardening, especially herb-gardening, creates even stronger bonds with the living, with family, friends and neighbours. My beds are full of plants given to me as Christmas or birthday presents or grown from cuttings and rootlets taken from other people's gardens. There is a great joy in going about thinking, 'There's Adrian's oregano, Val's sage and tansy, Dan and Karen's lavenders, Leonie's tarragon and lemon balm, Ruth's basil and lady's mantle, Jane's mint …' And many more who can rest assured their plants remind me of the donors every time I step outside the door.

The future, of course, is uncertain. It may be that the second garden at Tara will eventually go the way of the first but something at least will remain, like the first owners' trees and bulbs. With luck what I have put together—with a great deal of help, I may say, from John McGuinness, Dennis Tilyard and others—will go on thriving from season to season giving growing pleasure for many years to come and creating a living link between generations.

Motley crew rise to the occasion

Accuse Margaret Scott of deliberately making a well-considered, thoroughly sensible decision and I suspect she will interpret it as a severe insult and an attack upon her self image. Suggest politely that she is perhaps being a little impulsive, impractical and extravagant, hint that for a person in her dire health circumstances she is behaving in a risky, even unwise manner and she is on home turf. Her eyes lights up, the corners of her mouth form a barely perceptible smile of satisfaction and she shuffles down into her chair in the manner of an echidna anchoring itself to the ground.

Any suggestion that Margaret should abandon the blackened, damp and tangled mess that had been her beloved Tara, and move to a sensible little unit in Hobart, close to the hospital and services was met with this immovable determination. Margaret's life had been cleansed by fire once before in '67 and she understood the process. She was comfortable with the unpredictable nature of change and was determined to make it work for her.

I have mercifully never been summoned by the Queen, by Mother Teresa or by Don Corleone, but I cannot imagine any of them being harder to refuse than Margaret Scott in need of a builder. Not that she was pushy, mind you—quite the opposite. A polished combination of politeness, consideration, enthusiasm and, of course, flattery. I knew the instant she asked that I would do it, even though I had no idea how I would find the time. I have to say I was honoured to have been asked.

Margaret had already decided that she did not want to recreate Tara; it would have been virtually impossible anyway. The insurance money would not come anywhere near. She knew the bones of what she wanted—basically small and simple; barely more than a room for Margaret with a bathroom ... and a study, of course ... Oh, and able to fit a large library ... and with a separate area including a second bathroom that could accommodate family members and their children ... or friends ... and the odd group of writers ... and a large central space where everybody could get together, which would, of course, need to include a decent-sized kitchen to cater for large family gatherings or said writers groups, who could all sit together at the twenty-seat dining table ... OK, fourteen seat.

To these 'basic requirements' we started adding bits: A large deck with cantilevered roof connecting all areas and incorporating the foundation walls of Tara. A cool, south-facing conservatory, north-facing windows for winter sun, double glazing and lofty ceilings. We messed around with a number of different configurations of all of these elements and in the finish settled on a design that we had no hope of building for the budget. Absolutely no hope.

Margaret's enthusiasm and decisiveness are a delight to work with. I was fretting about sending her broke, finding ways to cut corners, make changes, but she had seen the model I made for her and loved it. 'Just go ahead, I'm sure we'll manage. Now, what colours will we paint living room?' Sapphire Blue, as it turned out and go ahead we did, but only after many animated, exhausting and sometimes hilarious sessions thrashing out the details. Margaret is passionate about colour and detail, jumping ahead to create finished interiors while I was still obsessively fussing over the basic structure, proportions and window placements. Having established that, in order to build the house, Margaret was prepared to live in an empty shell, dress in rags and sell her soul to the devil (assuming he did not already hold a mortgage over it), we sent the plans off to the council and set about finding a team to put it together.

We ended up with an excellent group of workers, including some of the best tradesmen in the area. However, it was possibly more than coincidence that Margaret's taste for the bizarre was reflected in the random collection of personalities on the job. Imagine morning tea in a small shed with a peace-loving, ageing hippy, a ranting right-wing reactionary, a militant (at least verbally) greenie, a surfer (only there when the wind was wrong), a pommie unionist, a gentleman of gay persuasion, an ex-chicken farmer and Basil Fawlty. What more can I say, except it was a mysteriously harmonious team that slogged away to make Margaret Scott's new house.

Most people who have built their own house will tell you it can be an exhausting, destructive business. Paradoxically, the closer to completion the more devastating can be the effects upon stress levels, health, relationships and self-esteem. Mention the word 'tradesman' and blood pressure will rise, hands shake involuntarily and eyes cast around for the nearest escape route. This was not the case for Margaret, in fact the opposite was true. When we started I have to say she looked grey and unwell, but the more seriously we became entangled in the design and building process the better she looked. Important decisions were made, reversed and re-made with remarkable ease, and all of the workers were treated to a dose of her trademark enthusiasm and flattery, even as she signed over large chunks of her cheque account to them. Whenever she visited the site it was always: 'I love it, I just love it.' Consequently the job had a positive atmosphere and Margaret received good value for money.

I am writing about Margaret, not her house, so I will spare the reader the story of the actual construction. The house certainly did not magically appear overnight as happens in the suburbs, but the way it grew and ripened as small changes and final decisions were made reflects the flexibility with which the whole project was undertaken. I am intrigued by the way it came about. One could not say that at all stages Margaret held a tight rein on developments, or even wanted to. At times she may have barely grasped the intricacies of construction, but she had the faith to give people freedom to do what they were good at, adding her own skills to the mix where needed.

Margaret got her house nearly on budget, actually improved her health, probably made a good investment, gave a lot of people work and satisfaction and, I suspect, further enriched her own remarkable life throughout the process. That, I am afraid to say, is thoroughly sensible decision making by anybody's standards.

Peter Rigozzi
Cabinetmaker, builder, designer

Peel back
the layers

Perhaps because smells are so evocative of the past, the onion, more than other less pungent vegetables, induces recollections of childhood. Whenever I make French onion soup or quiche lorraine I'm reminded of men on bicycles—exotic figures with berets and moustaches who, in the late 1930s, appeared every year in England and pedalled through the city streets selling strings of onions from door to door. They were said to come from Brittany but their onions were spoken of as Spanish. Watching my mother count out money at the front door, I used to think of the nursery rhyme about the King of Spain's daughter:

I had a little nut tree and nothing would it bear But a silver apple and a golden pear … The King of Spain's daughter came to visit me And all because of my little nut tree.

The pinkish sheen of the onions from the land of the sightseeing princess seemed touched with the fairytale lustre of the nut tree's fruit. And four or five onions from a string made a magical treat. My mother used to bake them, along with a few potatoes in their jackets, by putting them in the hot ashes under the sitting-room grate. When they were cooked we used to split them open, cover them with butter and eat our supper by firelight. It was the only kind of meal that we were allowed to eat without sitting up at the dining table and using knives and forks.

Probably my mother put up with these onion picnics because they were an effective way of getting children to eat what was good for them. Onions, which have been cultivated since at least the time of the Egyptian pharaohs, are, after all, packed with nutritious minerals and protein.

They are supposed to cleanse the blood and, for centuries, have been prized as a remedy for all sorts of ills ranging from toothache to indigestion. In the sixteenth century they were thought, rather oddly, to have both aphrodisiac and soporific properties or, as Andrew Boord put it in his *Dyetary of Helth,* 'to promote a man to veneryous acts and to sompnolence'. I doubt, though, that my mother had come across this idea. Like many other vegetables, onions have a host of namesakes— plants or other genera such as bog onion, the flowering fern *(Osmunda regalis);* dog's onion, otherwise known as the Star of Bethlehem; and the sea onion *(Urginea maritima)* which, like the true-blue onion, has been credited with curative powers. A remedy published in 1607 advises sufferers from boils to make up an ointment from 'the juice of asses dung, and of sea onions beat to powder'. And then, of course, there is onionweed, a plant that can make a devoted gardener turn as white as its deceptively pretty flower. It spreads like wildfire, collapses after flowering into a slimy mulch that kills everything else around it, and is almost impossible to eradicate. It multiplies by forming hundreds of tiny balls on the parent root so that, whatever you do, a few rogue bulblets always escape to lie low in your soil, ready to emerge jeeringly in the spring. I have a friend who once telephoned the Department of Agriculture to get advice on eliminating onionweed, and was told that the best plan was to move house.

As well as being associated with this mixed bag of plants, the genuine onion *(Allium cepa)* has been linked with a weird and wonderful collection of objects and ideas. The Latin word 'union', from which 'onion' derives, means both the edible rounded bulb and a kind of large pearl, so that it's not surprising to find pearls referred to as 'onions' in English from time to time.

Then in nineteenth century thieves' slang, 'onion' came to mean a seal worn on a watch-chain. The watch, attached to a middle button by a chain, went in one waistcoat pocket. A locket or something similar attached to the same button by a second chain went in another pocket, while the onions or seals dangled in a bunch over the wearer's midriff. Quite often the whole lot—watchcase, locket, chains and even some of the onions—were made of gold and constituted a rich prize for any thief wily enough to find a way of untangling the owner from his property.

'Onion' has also been used to denote various knobs or lumps, especially the painful kind that sometimes develop on feet. In 1785 a medical man called Low published *A Scientific Inquiry into the Causes of Corns, Warts, Onions and other Painful or Offensive Cutaneous Excrescences*, while *The Hull Advertiser* of April seventeen 1802 offered the services of an expert in the eradication of 'Corns, Onions or Nails growing into the Quick'—a man, it might be said, who knew his onions.

Just when onions changed into bunions is unclear. The practice of referring to swellings on the feet as onions died hard because the similarity between the vegetable and the footlump went beyond mere knobbiness. As a manual of surgery printed in 1846 remarked, 'The onion (or bunion) has a large base, and several layers of epidermis (like the layers of an onion) adhering to the skin in several points.'

The way in which the onion is made up of concentric layers, together with its tear-inducing properties, has given it a queerly paradoxical reputation. On the one hand it is associated with getting at the truth, with stripping away pretence and protective covering until you arrive at the heart of the matter—which may, if you pick hard enough, be absolutely nothing. On the other hand, because an onion can bring on weeping that has nothing to do with grief, it has often been linked with hypocrisy or fake emotion. Ibsen uses onion-peeling as an attempt to find truth in his verse drama, *Peer Gynt*, when Peer, grown old and disenchanted, likens himself to an onion and rips away at the layers that represent the roles he has played in his life. Conversely, the eighteenth century writer John Wolcott gives an acid description of Master Broadbrim who 'por'd o'er his father's will, and drop'd the onion'd tear', while, later, Bernard Shaw refers to 'the undertaker's handkerchief, duly onioned with some pathetic phrase'.

But when all is said and done, whether we associate the onion with pearls or bunions, unvarnished truth or crocodile tears, it remains for most of us the tastiest and most versatile of vegetables. Sydney Smith praised it for animating salad but failed to point out that it can do the same for almost any savoury dish—soup, stew, omelette, quiche, sauce, curry … the list is virtually endless. You can serve an onion raw, fried, baked, stewed, battered or steamed. You can mince, chop or slice it or cook it whole. You can pickle it, make it into marmalade or even 'pearl' it—which means, I'm told, stripping an onion down to the size of a marble and tossing it in hot butter until it takes on the faintly translucent look of a jewel fit for a queen.

And onions, for all their sumptuousness, are not hard to grow. Given reasonably good soil you can grow them in most climates, provided you choose the right varieties, but they are most at home in places where the winter is quite cold. In Tasmania, for instance, they have flourished for decades and, since the arrival of the first white settlers in 1803, have played a humble but significant part in the island's history.

As many readers will know, the practice of assigning convicts to free masters came to an end in 1840 and was replaced by a new 'probation' system. This meant that every convict transported to Van Diemen's Land was sent off to join a gang engaged on public works. These gangs were housed in outstations well away from the settled parts of the state. The Tasman Peninsula, where the Port Arthur penal settlement had already been established, was considered an excellent site for a string of probation stations—Flinders Bay; Norfolk Bay (Taranna); Cascades (Koonya); Impression Bay (Premaydena); Salt Water River; the Coal Mines (Plunkett Point); and Wedge Bay (Nubeena).

Today at Premaydena little remains of the building that once stretched away on either side of the present road to Nubeena, but in 1845 over six hundred convicts and staff were housed there, busily employed in providing various supplies for the Convict Department. Timber was cut and milled, some of which was shipped across Norfolk Bay for use as pit-props in the mines at Plunkett Point. According to Comptroller-General William Champ, timber was also used in 'the manufacture of carts, wheelbarrows and other implements required by the Department'.

And as well as all this, the station produced a quantity of food. In late 1896 Charles Joseph Latrobe visited Impression Bay, which had by then been turned into an Invalid Station, and reported rather sourly, 'Of the land in cultivation the soil is very indifferent and will not produce anything beyond a few vegetables or hops, in the preparation of which the invalids may be suitably employed.'

Now this is rather odd because about eighteen months earlier, when the station had been buzzing with activity, a list of foodstuffs harvested in the previous year had been drawn up. It included 156 bushels of wheat and barley; 15,292lbs of cabbages; 9,243lbs of carrots; 26 tons of turnips and—yes—2, 167lbs of onions. A few vegetables?

Onions figure in another story from the convict period—the tale recounted by Ian Brand in his book *The Escape*. This is my favourite convict story. It has everything—tragedy, humour, suspense and a remarkable hero in the person of Thomas Walker of Deptford, five feet nine inches tall, with light brown hair and grey eyes. Walker began his career, it seems, as a sailor. When he was only sixteen years old he was sentenced to seven years transportation for housebreaking and arrived in Van Diemen's Land in September 1825. He ran foul of the authorities only a few weeks after starting work on the Government Farm at New Town (25 lashes for disobedience of orders, insolence and neglect of duty), and from that time on was hardly ever out of trouble. Looking through his record one gets the impression that nobody knew quite what to do with him. He was sentenced to numerous sets of lashes, rising from 25 to 150 and totalling in the end 1006. He was sent to various chain gangs, to Maria Island and to Port Arthur. His sentence was repeatedly extended, he was put on short rations and worked in irons, but nothing seemed to have the desired effect. Whatever his punishment, Thomas Walker kept on trying to escape.

In April 1838 he was returned to Port Arthur where he became a member of the crew of one of the settlement's whale boats. On the morning of February 13, 1839, Walker and seven other convicts from the boat crews went to the slip immediately below the military barracks and guard tower, climbed into the Commandant's whaleboat and, before anyone realised what was happening, shot off towards the open sea. That night, after a long and fruitless sea chase, the Commandant, Captain O'Hara Booth, sat down in some embarrassment to write his report: 'It is with no little degree of mortification and regret I have to report for the information of His Excellency the Lieutenant Governor the escape from the Settlement in a Six Oar'd Whale Boat (commonly known as the Commandant's Whaleboat) the eight persons named in the margin …'

A full-scale hunt was mounted. The Government schooner, *Eliza*, a brigantine, and two parties of constables in a whale boat set out from Hobart, while O'Hara Booth despatched a second brig, the *Isabella*, from Port Arthur. The pursuers discovered that Walker's party had landed on Bruny Island, purloined a pig and crossed the D'Entrecasteaux Channel to Southport. A posse rushed to Recherche Bay only to find that the runaways had raided a whaling station and again vanished into the blue just four hours earlier. The *Eliza* sailed on to Port Davey, the *Isabella* doubled back to Bruny Island, while still another government ship, the *Shamrock*, was ordered to search the north and west coasts. Yet, even though, at one point, the *Eliza* passed so close to one of Walker's hide-outs that the convicts saw the lookouts on her cross-trees, no trace could be found of the Commandant's whaleboat.

The Walker Gang made two raids on a settlement at Port Davey and then moved round to the east coast. Often they pulled their boat into hiding on the shore throughout the day and went forward at night, descending from time to time on some settler's home in order to replenish their supplies. Always, on these occasions, they behaved in a way that startled their victims and baffled their pursuers. At one place they paid for all they took and Walker lent his host a book, at others they were careful to leave their victims adequate supplies or left corn in place of flour. They avoided violence and, in one witness's words, 'committed no outrage on anyone'.

One East Coast farmer, Mr Davis, was actually fooled into believing that Walker was in charge of a party hunting for the escapees. 'The men,' he said, 'looked so orderly and were so neatly dressed, that I had no reason to disbelieve them.' He asked Walker to join him at dinner and thought his conduct at table 'much above that of the lower order'. And what did they take from the settlers? Clothes, tobacco, guns—though they seem never to have used them on anything other than kangaroos—dried meat, flour, tea and various other foodstuffs including, on more than one occasion, a quantity of onions.

With their gear, including the onions, piled in their boat, the party went on to

Flinders Island where, for some reason, a convict called Nicholas Lewis was left behind. The remaining seven crossed Bass Strait and, rather strangely, were recaptured in New South Wales by a posse from the cutter, *Prince George*. Sad to relate, Walker and one of his comrades, Henry Dixon, died in gaol before they could be brought to trial. Five others were sentenced to life imprisonment on Norfolk Island, but one, John Thomas, a Liverpool labourer only five feet one inch tall, was mysteriously discharged. Could he have been the Judas who slipped the word to the captain of the *Prince George*?

The story leaves other questions hanging in the air. How did Walker and Dixon die? Above all, how did a man who had known little but the chain gang and the lash for almost half his thirty-two years manage to remain so humorous and humane? One feels that, if Fate had dealt Tom Walker a different hand, the spirit, daring and ingenuity that kept him and his men ahead of their pursuers for three months might have brought him fame as an admiral, a general or a great explorer. As it is, his story deserves to be more widely known, so that I hope readers will forgive the fact that it is only faintly flavoured with onions. After all, as Sydney Smith pointed out, one of the onion's greatest services to a dish is to lurk in its depths, 'scarce suspected', imparting a subtle flavour to the whole.

Dear Margaret,

the fond beginning of a screed
I've meant to write, put off
by lack of ink, the Royal Mail's
daily losses or, notably,

the interference of a song
called 'Dear Margaret' by The Kinks—
even though it's a decade since
I've heard it played. It is raucous,

repetitive, commercial, crude.
None of this list of qualities
could I associate with you.
There's also certainty the song lacks wit

unless like the average critic
I don't get it. But by now you'll ask,
why did he listen to the thing?
Well, that'd be rougher to justify

than the long delay in writing.
Meantime this, dear Margaret, comes
with a promise to share some news,
unimpeded by any lame excuse

and, right now, in this dark deep-freeze,
a wish for summer light, the kind that floods,
where there was ash, your amazing house,
newly risen, unique, exemplary.

Andrew Sant
Poet

All seated round the tub

On 24 April, 1803, HMS *Calcutta*, the first British vessel to carry a consign-
ment of convicts to Van Diemen's Land, set out on her voyage to Australia.
Among the 308 transported men on board were several who were to make their
mark in the new colonies, John Fawkner, father of John Pascoe Fawkner, a founder
of Melbourne, Francis Barnes, who printed the colony's first newspaper, and, per-
haps most remarkable of all, the forger, James Grove, whose wide-ranging talents,
subtle wit and breathtaking cheek placed him in a class of his own. Grove, after
being condemned to death at Warwick, managed to get his sentence commuted to
transportation for life by supplying the British government with interesting hints
on the detection of forged Bank of England notes. Thereafter he was treated with
every consideration, driven to the *Calcutta* in a carriage, provided with a pleasant
cabin which he was allowed to share with his wife and child, and left in peace to
while away the voyage by teaching his four-year-old son to read from *The Pilgrim's
Progress.*

On arriving in Van Diemen's Land, Grove at once noticed a lack of any equiva-
lent of the modern picture postcard. He dashed off the first recorded sketch of
Hobart Town and was soon besieged by colonists wanting similar drawings to send
home to friends and relations. This was just the beginning. And in his spare mo-
ments, Grove established a soap-making operation. With his usual skill in ingra-
tiating himself with the right people, he sent a presentation parcel of his best soap
to the wife of Governor King in New South Wales. Unhappily James Grove died
young, dosed, some say, with arsenic by a jealous rival. Had he survived, Hobart
might have become the soapbowl of the southern hemisphere, as famous for its fine
soaps as the European centres of Castile and Bologna had been in the past or the
producers of Pears and Lifebuoy were to be in the future.

How did Grove pick up the art of soap-making? Perhaps, one day, glancing
up from *The Pilgrim's Progress* or a quick sketch of Mount Wellington, he noticed
his wife doing something queer with wood ash and the fat of a kangaroo. Per-
haps, searching through such books as he could find in the infant colony, he came
upon the eighteenth century dictionary which states, 'For black Soap, tis made with
strong lye… and whale or fish-oil, commonly called Train-Oil'. Lots of soap-mak-
ing lore like this was available in Grove's time. By the first decade of the nineteen-
thth century soap had been use in western Europe for a very long time. Basically
soap is made by combining some kind of oil or fat with some alkaline substance
such as potash or caustic soda. Some claim that it was invented by the Phoenicians
around 600BC, others that the Tartars thought it up and that it came filtering into
Europe with the caravans of merchandise that travelled the ancient trade routes

from the East. ('Have you tried our new yak-butter soap, madam? Matchless for the complexion!')

The Romans spotted soap in the Teutonic regions. Pliny, the Roman historian, mentions soap *(sapo)* made by boiling goat fat with wood ashes, and the remains of a soap-factory have been found at Pompeii. In England the Anglo-Saxons made soap. From their time onwards English records and works of literature are spattered with soapy references. Soap turns up in the York Minster Fabric Rolls of 1371, the fifteenth century Coventry Corpus Christi plays, and reports of cases heard in the Star Chamber in 1515. In 1592, the Elizabethan poet Thomas Lodge came up with the wise adage: 'Who washeth the Asses eares, loseth both his sope and his Labour.' By the 1640s soap, which could only be made under patent, was big business in London.

Despite all this, English soap was rather looked down upon by the connoisseur. It was Spain, Italy and Southern France, where olive oil and soda were readily obtainable, that came to been seen as producers of the finest and most delicate soap deluxe. In the soap houses of Lambeth and Westminster the usual ingredients were rather coarse—animal fats and lye, a caustic liquid produced by straining water through wood ash held in a sieve or 'lye-dropper'. Yet English soap, right up until after the time of James Grove, remained expensive, a commodity reserved for the well-to-do.

Thrifty housewives made their own soap, but it was a fiddly business. Having made your lye, you had to boil it up until it reached exactly the right concentration for soap-making. Then you had to simmer it with the oil or melted fat and, after about three hours, throw in salt. This caused the mixture to separate into two layers—soap curd on top, brine and glycerol underneath. The curd was then creamed off into moulds, coloured according to taste—beetroot juice for pink, spinach for green, perfumed with herbs such as lavender and left to cool. The poor fought shy of soap-making because they needed all the animal fats they could get for food and for their tallow candles and rushlights. Sometimes they used herbs such as soapwort as a laundry aid. More often they did what people have done for centuries all over the world—trampled the wash in a tub of plain water, bashed it against the rocks in a stream or whacked it clean with a club known as a 'beetle'. Occasionally they used lye on its own to whiten clothes, a practice which, in some areas, survived well into the twentieth century. In her account of growing up on Flinders Island in the 1920s and 30s, Ida West describes how she and her family carried water home from a well and then made lye with ashes to bleach their laundry.

In the late eighteenth century, soap-making took a great leap forward when a French chemist, Nicholas Leblanc, found a cheap way of making soda from brine. For a time though, the price of soap in Britain remained high and the stuff retained its sweet elusive scent of luxury—or so, one imagines, James Grove must have felt when he packed up a batch of his wares to send to Mrs King. He may also have realised that in the recent past soap had acquired other even more seductive qualities, exactly calculated to appeal to a Governor's lady in a remote corner of the British Empire. It had taken on an odour of righteousness and was rapidly gaining the status of a civilising influence.

The conviction that dirt is linked with evil, and cleanliness with virtue is deeply ingrained in the culture of western Europe. Christian literature is full of images of souls, spotted and stained with sin, washed and rendered pure by penitence and redemption. Yet up until the late 1700s people seem to have been content to take all this in a figurative sense and, even when they could afford soap, saw no need to demonstrate the purity of their souls by constantly scrubbing their bodies. Eighteenth century satirists, though often rather grubby men, were always poking fun at the fashionable lady's tendency to use paint and false hair in preference to soap and water. 'She drawls her words and waddles in her pace, Unwashed her hands, and much be snuffed her face,' writes one.

Things started to change when John Wesley, in a sermon on dress, reminded his flock that 'cleanliness is next to godliness'. As Evangelical piety began to percolate through all classes of society, white linen, clean hands and well-scrubbed surroundings were seen more and more as evidences of virtue and respectability. The poor were divided into the 'deserving' and the 'undeserving' according to the level of cleanliness they managed to achieve. Certain beggars, realising this, took to scrubbing their children.

As the missionary zeal for cleanliness tightened its grip, more and more philanthropists were advancing upon the lower classes with a Bible in one hand and a cake of soap in the other. Edwin Chadwick, born in 1800 and trained to wash himself daily, grew up to play a major role in reforming the Old Poor Law, motivated, according to G M Young, by 'a desire to wash the people of England all over, every day, by administrative order'. Florence Nightingale, setting out for the Crimea, warned her nurses, 'The strongest will be wanted at the wash-tub.'

There was a good deal of sense in this, of course. As the Industrial Revolution rolled on, the slums of the larger cities were rapidly becoming deathtraps, crammed with people living in indescribable filth. The insanitary condition of the Crimean hospitals was doing more than the onslaughts of the enemy towards wiping out the British army. The trouble was, perhaps, that the British had started to equate soap with civilisation. They carried it all over the Empire. Missionaries were not content simply to convert the heathen. He or she had to be kept in a high state of cleanliness. Yet there were some who felt that there was something disagreeable about the feel of soapy things—something slippery. They christened Bishop Wilberforce 'Soapy Sam' and took to equating flattery with soap. Even today a person who butters somebody up is sometimes said to be laying on soft soap. One can't help wondering whether Mrs King, on opening her present from Hobart, suspected for a moment that James Grove was adept not only at making soap but also at applying the soft variety.

Weathering passionate differences

Being a relative newcomer to the Tasman Peninsula where Margaret lives, I have not had the privilege of 'length of time' to qualify my friendship with her as being one of many, many years. However, after a double dozen or so encounters over breakfast, lunch, shared radio interviews, afternoon teas and community gatherings in the past eight years, and having the fortune to observe her in conversation 'listening' and then contributing wisely and succulently to the topic at hand, I have developed a deep fondness for the wizened character that is the elder, Margaret Scott. Even her smoking beneath the finger wagging hum of the oxygen bottles has been one of endearment rather than despair.

A true test of any friendship lies in its ability to weather storms and passionate differences. During the run up to the Ten Days on the Island festival in 2003, Margaret and I held sharply different views on whether artists should boycott the event because of Forestry Tasmania's involvement in it. As in a hot fire where garbage burns, yet steel is tempered, our friendship became stronger through this debate. The explanation lies simply in the fact that even though Margaret willingly and with force engaged in dialogue over the pros and cons of the boycott, her characteristic heartfelt constant respect for the other person (in this case, me) never waned. Out of this, our friendship deepened.

When Margaret presents herself, her views, to the world, there is never a sense of one-upmanship. This is the hallmark of Margaret Scott. Rather than using her extreme intelligence and command of the language to subdue anyone, she couples a clean wit with a keen and knowing interest in the alternative viewpoint to seduce them.

How many of us have fallen hopelessly in love with the beauty of this woman; desirous for the chance of just one more meeting with her around the kitchen table?

Peter Adams
Sculptor

Medley of strange contrasts

There are signs abroad that apples are coming back, that Tasmania will once again be a place of orchards, a true Apple Isle. This is heartening because, for years, the ghost of the once bustling apple industry has haunted the island, sighing with the wind through abandoned sheds, lingering round the derelict piers where in times gone by mountains of cases were hurried aboard the steamers bound for Hobart. Older people in the Huon Valley or on the Tasman Peninsula point sadly at the bare paddocks, which all through the thirties, forties and fifties were thick with trees. Poking around in old cottages you find bits of apple case everywhere—behind the meat safe, under the wallpaper, patching the dunny floor. Even the ply on the back of my blackwood desk is stamped 'for export only'. And it'll be good to see the apples back, because they suit Tasmania. This most intriguing of fruits with its curiously contrasted associations—desirable, sinister, homely and splendid—is a fitting emblem for an island whose history, landscapes and people are themselves a fascinating medley of strange contrasts.

When I was young I was surprised by the frequency with which apples crop up in stories. Greek myths are full of them. Take the tale of the fleet-footed Atalanta who refused to marry any suitor unless he could beat her in a race. Milanion, much smitten by the beautiful sprinter, appealed to Aphrodite, goddess of love. 'Take these three golden apples,' said the goddess, 'and whenever Atalanta starts to draw ahead, toss one of them in her path.' The plan worked like a charm. Atalanta, attracted by the shining fruits, kept stopping to gather them so that Milanion managed to reach the winning post well ahead of her. (I regret to say they didn't live happily ever after but were subsequently both turned into lions by a god less sympathetic than Aphrodite.) Then there was the apple of discord which Paris, Prince of Troy, awarded the goddess of love as first prize in a divine beauty contest. Needless to say, the unplaced goddesses were not too impressed by Paris's judgement, so that he too came to a less than fortunate end.

In Genesis, of course, the apple is at the heart of the drama of the Fall of Man—the forbidden fruit that Eve plucks from the Tree of Knowledge of Good and Evil. There are still more apples in fairy stories—the one used to poison Snow White, for instance—and in legends like the tale of William Tell who was forced to shoot at an apple placed on the head of his young son.

More recently apples have featured in all kinds of novels ranging from Stevenson's *Treasure Island,* in which young Jim Hawkins hears mutiny plotted while hidden in an apple barrel, to Bessie Marchant's *The Apple Lady,* set among the orchards of the Huon Valley.

Poets as well as novelists, have often turned to apples for inspiration. In an age when bad teeth and bad breath were all too common, Chaucer described Alison, the alluring heroine of 'The Miller's Tale' as having a mouth as 'sweet as a hoard of apples stored in hay or heather'. Later Andrew Marvell in 'The Garden' exclaims:

What wondrous life is this I lead! Ripe apples drop about my head...

Keats speaks of Autumn conspiring with the sun 'to bend with apples the mossed cottage-trees'; Yeats dreams of plucking 'The silver apples of the moon/The golden apples of the sun'; Drinkwater yearns over his 'Moonwashed apples of wonder'; and Coleridge, according to Charles Lamb, thought 'that a man cannot have a pure mind who refuses apple dumplings'.

Apples also figure prominently in all sorts of games and ancient customs from the old sport of 'bobbing' or ducking for apples in a tub of water to the Cornish practice of giving Allan or Allantide apples as luck-bringers. If you ate your Allan apple on Hallowe'en you'd have good luck throughout the coming year, and if a young girl slept with her apple under her pillow she was supposed to dream of her future husband. In Gloucestershire, where I grew up, we preferred to sleep undisturbed by lumps in our pillows but we enjoyed finding apples, along with oranges and half-crowns, stuffed in the toes of our Christmas stockings—the last treats to emerge after all the presents had been pulled out. At the same time, back in Gloucestershire, where we used to shake the trees in the orchard and stuff the fallen fruit into sacks to make cider, I did sometimes wonder why people got so worked up about apples. I thought Atalanta was a bit of a goose to go shooting off the track after a Beauty of Bath or a Blenheim Orange—unless, of course, she secretly fancies Milanion and wanted him to win the race. As for Eve! Everyone knew you shouldn't talk to strange snakes. It enraged me to think I'd been born a miserable sinner just because the silly woman couldn't go past a Worcester Pearmain. Since those childhood days I've tried to look more calmly at the matter, turning over in my mind the cultural significance of apples in general, but to some extent I'm baffled by this weirdly ambivalent fruit.

For centuries apples have been commended as wholesome. 'An apple a day keeps the doctor away' is an old maxim. In the Tudor period it was held that toasted apples were 'holsome when the stomake is weake'. And 'apple-cheeked', much more than 'rosy', suggests cheery cleanliness and good health. Apples have also long been recognised as attractive-looking things, usually with a pleasant, sweet taste. So far so good. But in myth and folklore apples become infinitely more than wholesome, pretty, delicious pieces of fruit. They represent the acme of desirability, the supreme treat or prize. Often, like the apples guarded by a dragon in the garden of the Hesperides, as well as Atalanta's apples and the apple of discord, they are described as golden. Equally often they are linked in some way with a woman or goddess, with beauty, love and sex, with doting on 'the apple of one's eye'.

One explanation of the value placed on apples in Northern Europe is simply that until quite recently most people existed on a fairly dreary diet. The choice of sweet things available to all but the very rich was limited and, while a number of fruits—apricots, for instance, but nothing as exotic as bananas—could be had in summer, it was only pears and apples from those 'mossed cottage trees' that could be stored away for the winter.

Since apples are sweet, luscious, round and bestow moments of sensuous ecstasy, it's not surprising that they should be so constantly linked with women and love. One of the sexiest scenes I've ever seen on film consisted simply of two lovers sitting at a table, eating apples at each other. Moreover, from a male point of view, apples may be associated with sex because they have been emblems of conquest. Colonists arriving in the new territory often stake their claim by clearing and building, but typically, they also establish their presence by planting seeds brought from the homeland. The early annals of white settlement in Australia and of the American conquest of the West are full of the business of getting the grain into the ground—in the first place, of course, to avoid starvation, but also, it seems, to proclaim occupation, to turn the new home into something that looked and felt like the one the settlers had left behind. For British and American colonists there was nothing more reassuring than an expanse of waving corn—unless it was an apple tree. Once the apple trees were up and bearing, you knew you were really in charge, and like the trees, had put down roots. The British planted apple trees like flags. (Bligh, for instance, put in a few on Bruny Island when he called there in 1788.) In America, John Chapman, or Johnny Appleseed, has become a national hero for his diligence in planting apple trees wherever he went, and it may be that New York is known as the Big Apple because it's the place where the national presence has grown tallest—a kind of super-tree laden with golden prizes.

But for all this, apples, like women in Judaeo-Christian tradition, have their dark side. As in the story of the Fall, they are wonderfully tempting. 'Apple-eating', meaning 'easily tempted', was once the word applied to 'foolish, credulous women', and 'apple squire' was a name given to pimps or tempters. But, of course, a fair outward appearance may well conceal corruption. The apple pie bed—unlike apple pie order—comes as a nasty surprise. 'The goodly apple rotten to the heart' is proverbial. Apples can be poisoned (witness Snow White) or bring danger, as with Hercules in the Hesperidean garden or Christina Rossetti's Laura who foolishly eats the magic fruit of the goblins. They can land you in the most appalling strife, as in the case of Eve or the Prince of Troy. Then there are those strange Apples of Sodom or Dead Sea Fruit, described by Josephus—and later Byron—as beautiful to see but dissolving when grasped into smoke and ashes.

At this point one feels bound to leap to the defence of the Granny Smith and her kind. I've met codling moth in an apple but never ashes. Perhaps the Dead Sea Fruit aren't apples at all. Perhaps the golden apples of myth were another type of fruit altogether. Maybe Atalanta went scurrying after a trio of grapefruit and Eve reached forth her 'rash hand', as Milton calls it, for a Jaffa orange. The name 'apple' has, after all, been slung around pretty freely at times and appended to lots of fruits that are nothing like apples. The pomegranate was once called an 'apple punic' and the tomato a 'love apple'. There are also pineapples, oak apples, custard apples, thorn apples and many more such pretenders. The French *pomme de terre* (potato) means 'apple of the earth' and pome-citron is an old name for citrus fruit.

However that may be, one can only hope that as the orchards begin to spread across the Tasmanian valleys once more, their fruit, though rich in ancient and varied associations, will be free of taints, traps and ashes, tempting us into nothing worse than a few too many Ladies in the Snow.

Wiped out by parrots

Caroline Lurie set up Australian Literary Management in Melbourne in 1980. John Bryson, an ALM author, mentioned to Caroline that Margaret Scott was working on a 'marvellous novel'; Caroline wrote to Margaret and signed her up in 1987. A decade later I joined Caroline as a partner to open a Sydney branch of ALM, and we worked together until 1993 when Caroline decided to retire from agency life and I became the owner.

Margaret is one of my most cherished authors. She is a writer of subtle and complex insights woven together by a mature talent, and I feel she has made an important contribution to Australian literature. But above all she is an optimist, a person of great cheer even through some very dark times.

As an agent it is always a pleasure to let an author know of a good deal just made and I've had many occasions over the years to do that with Margaret. But there are also difficult times; times for example when you have to phone an author with news that is not quite what they were hoping for. In 1988 Caroline wrote to Margaret with the news that she'd had no luck in securing any agents in the UK to represent Margaret's *The Baby Farmer*. Caroline felt sure they would 'live to eat their words', she said, and apologised for the cliché. Margaret's response was 'I like clichés like "live to eat their words". They conjure up very satisfying pictures such as you and me quaffing champagne while the offending agents chew miserably through acres of paper sandwiches'. Writers don't often take bad news with such good cheer as that; which is why it is always a delight to ring and chat with her on the phone, even if part of that call is to relay a (very occasional) rejection.

Margaret's poetry is so good that she seems to me sometimes like a wonderful poet who occasionally stoops to prose and manages to write it excellently well. My husband John has spent a lifetime in the salt mines of verse, and he says he ranks Margaret's poems very high: a little like A D Hope, he says, but she wears her learning more gracefully; as colourful as Slessor, but with a warmer human touch. To me her poems have a dramatic flow and a bright verbal patterning that seem effortless, but both, of course, are the product of decades of patient labour.

My familiarity, of course, rests mainly with Margaret's literary work and her numerous speaking engagements. The latter was something that arose quite a few years after her retirement from university life. And she was much sought after as an after-dinner speaker for conferences and charity events. The reason for Margaret's success in that area I believe was quite simple: she is one of the funniest women I know. Her wit and humour are legendary. Only recently when I spoke to her I asked how things were going. 'Oh, fine,' she said, 'but my poor neighbour has been completely wiped out by parrots.'

Margaret is one of the half-dozen people I have met who somehow make the journey through life a richer and a better experience.

Lyn Tranter
Literary agent

In a stew about porridge

Porridge—pronounced 'parritch' by some of its keenest fans—is not my favourite food. My mother used to serve it up for breakfast every morning in winter but the only thing about it that I ever really liked was the Scotsman on the coloured oatmeal packet. He was a brawny fellow with a bright, swirling kilt and he was holding up one arm as though he'd just thrown something heavy into the far distance—probably a caber, one of those poles or beams that are hurled hither and thither in Highland games. This Scotsman obviously doted on porridge, as do a number of my friends who seem convinced that the only way to face a wintry Tasmanian dawn is to shovel down a bowl or two of steaming oatmeal before venturing out into the sleet.

Porridge, of course, used to signify all kinds of mixtures that went far beyond a stew of oats and water. The word is actually an altered form of 'pottage' or 'poddish' and, as such, according to *The Oxford English Dictionary,* denoted 'pottage' or soup made by stewing vegetables, herbs or meat, often thickened with pot-barley or other farinaceous addition.

On February 25, 1660, Samuel Pepys noted in his famous diary that he had eaten some 'nettle porrige' which he found very good. And a medical journal of 1805 warns against using the herb 'fool's parsley' because 'some persons have been rendered delirious by eating porridge wherein it had been used instead of (ordinary) parsley'. Then there was plum-porridge, the forerunner of Christmas pudding, which seems to have been a thick soup made with dried fruits—especially dried plums or prunes, spices, wine, sugar and various other ingredients including, rather strangely, an occasional piece of beef or mutton. Another well-known dish was pease-porridge, a stodgy pea soup, likened by some to mud, and frequently eaten in Lent in place of meat. People seem to have got rather sick of it, especially when it was dished up cold. My mother, who grew up in Gloucestershire used to sing:

Pease-porridge hot,
Pease-porridge cold,
Pease-porridge in the pot
Nine days old!

In Shakespeare's play *The Tempest*, Alonso, grieving for his lost son, turns from a would-be comforter, saying 'prithee peace'. The heartless Sebastian, punning on 'peace' and 'pease', remarks in a sniggering aside to a friend: 'He receives comfort like cold porridge.' It's quite a clever simile, really. Stale pease-porridge served cold over and over again through Lent probably made a lot of people avert their faces with looks suggestive of deep personal grief.

Happily, so far as I know, cold pease-porridge is a thing of the past. A few non-water brews—Chinese rice-porridge, for instance—are still eaten in Australia; but for most inhabitants of the chillier states, porridge for breakfast this winter will mean hot oatmeal, associated not with Lenten fasting but with Scottish muscle. Quite when the Scots became addicted to porridge is unclear. Since oats are the hardiest of cereals and will grow where the climate is cold and the soil poor, they were cultivated in the Highlands of Scotland from very early times. In 1523, Lord Bemers remarked that it was a habit of Scotsmen to journey about with 'a lytle sacke full of oatmele' tied behind their saddles. This was a very sensible practice in wild and sometimes snowy country. By the middle of the eighteenth century, at least, oats had become the staple food of Scotland—or so Dr Johnson believed. His *Dictionary of the English Language* gives the following definition of oats: 'A grain which in England is generally given to horses, but in Scotland supports the people.' Yet when Johnson finally visited Scotland, years after the Dictionary had been published, nobody, it seems, offered him a single oat. By 1783, when Johnson and Boswell made their famous tour, great changes were afoot in Scotland. For over 70 years these changes would roll on, dividing the lairds from their clansmen, transforming the face of the Highlands, bringing terrible hardship to thousands of people, and exerting a lasting effect on the destinies of the colonies thousands of miles away from the Scottish glens. Through all this time, oats or porridge, the traditional food of the people, played a humble but significant part in the drama; right up until what was perhaps the very last act, played out—oddly enough—in a remote corner of the remote colony of Tasmania.

The changes began at Culloden in 1746 when Bonnie Prince Charlie's forces were defeated by the English army of the Duke of Cumberland. For centuries before the battle, society in the Highlands had remained largely feudal. Every laird lived surrounded by his clansmen, a host of tenants and subtenants who paid little or no rent for the land on which they grew their oats or herded their black cattle. Instead they were pledged to serve as fighting men when their laird summoned them to war. After Culloden, the Highland chieftains were stripped of much of their power. Clan warfare ceased and the lairds, reduced from warlords to landed gentry, began to turn their minds to other matters—some to improving their estates, some to high life in Edinburgh or London.

Whatever their tastes, nearly all were agreed that the lands that had once provided warriors must now be put to a different use. There was money to be made from running sheep, but before the glens could be turned into sheepruns the jumble of little farms and thousands of people who lived on them would have to go. In his book, *The Highland Clearances* (Penguin, 1969), John Prebble tells the story of how a whole population was gradually prised up and driven from its homeland. Many had their cabins burned over their heads. Whole communities, having watched their laird's officers tear down their homes, were left utterly destitute, with no shelter at all in the depths of winter. And when the people asked where they should go, the answer was always the same: To the emigrant ships! To make matters worse, these ships were often owned or chartered by unscrupulous speculators, intent on collecting as much passage money as they could for the smallest possible outlay. Despite government regulations designed to force shipmasters to provide adequate rations, a good many treated the law with contempt. Shipowners like William Allen of Leith ridiculed the Passenger Act of 1803 on finding that, for every child on board, he was supposed to carry a range of foodstuffs including 52 gallons of water and 36 pounds of oatmeal. Yet, at a time when sailing ships commonly took six weeks to make the voyage from Scotland to Canada, what sounds like an excessive amount of cereal actually pans out at about 400g (maybe two bowls of porridge) per child per day. With people like William Allen in charge, the Highlanders' children ended up, of course, with much less. If ships were delayed by bad weather, provisions sometimes shrank to next to nothing and the water, if it held out, turned sour. Inevitably, bad water, inadequate food and overcrowding brought disease, so that thousands of emigrants died of typhus, cholera or dysentery before ever setting foot in their promised land.

Matters were not much better when the victims of the Clearances provided their own food. Pamphlets were issued advising Highland families to lay in 'four stones of oatmeal and four of cutlings' (coarse porridge oats) while *The Inverness Courier* suggested that, for a voyage to Cape Breton Island, each grown person should carry aboard 'one boll (48 gallons) of oatmeal and another of potatoes'. Many, of course, were far too poor to secure anything like these quantities of food, yet it was only in the last years of the Highland Clearances that there was any concerted effort to assist the destitute to emigrate. The body that was to become The Highland and Island Emigration Society was set up in 1851, funded largely by public donations, with the aim of procuring 'help for those who wish to emigrate but have not the means of doing so'.

The Society, though it came too late to help most victims of the Clearances, did a good deal to ensure that the last Highlanders to be evicted from their homes left Britain in seaworthy ships, carrying adequate provisions for a long voyage. One such ship—the *Persian,* newly-built and fully provisioned by Messrs Wilson and Chambers of the White Star Line—sailed from Liverpool on July 26,1857. On board were 201 Highlanders—twenty-two families from Harris in the Outer Hebrides, where at one stage the army was called to remove the owner's subtenants, and thirteen families from Coll in the Inner Hebrides which lost half its population in the long-running drive to turn crofts into pastures for sheep. It's hard to know exactly when these thirty-five families left their islands. Certainly some had spent time in Glasgow before arriving in Liverpool. One can only say that, since the Clearances are usually seen as ending in 1854, the story of the *Persian* forms a sad little epilogue to the saga of eviction from the Highlands—and, since the *Persian* was bound for Hobart, that epilogue ended here in Tasmania.

Although there was no shortage of oatmeal and most other supplies on the *Persian,* the cooking facilities left much to be desired. On emigrant ships the steerage passengers usually formed groups, with one person from each group acting as cook for all the others, but sometimes this arrangement failed to solve the problem of overcrowding in the galley. Captain Kerr of the *Persian* remarked that 'great numbers of persons' were constantly in the galley to get things cooked, or to cook for themselves,' while one of the emigrants complained that the 'galley was too small and not adapted to the job'. He went on to explain: 'we made oatmeal, and that was made into porridge … for breakfast, but we found that people did not wash their cans in taking water to make it, and thus we found tea-leaves in the porridge, and we did not use it.'

Unhappily, the Highlanders on the *Persian* were to face trials very much graver than tea-leaves in the porridge. One of their number, Anne MacKinnon from Coll, had contracted typhus in Glasgow. She took to her berth as soon as she came on board, was carried to the ship's hospital and died only three weeks after leaving Liverpool. Then the disease began to spread. By the time the *Persian* dropped anchor in the Derwent at the end of October, six had died of the fever, four more were to die before the sick could be brought ashore, and over 20 others were seriously ill.

The problem facing the colony was—where to send the *Persian?* Very rapidly it was decided to turn the Convict Probation Station at Impression Bay (now Premaydena) on the Tasman Peninsula into a makeshift hospital and quarantine station. A medical officer was appointed, stores were rushed to the site, the *Persian* was towed to Impression Bay and bit by bit the passengers and crew—first the healthy and then the sick—were installed in the dormitories, mess-halls and cottages of the former Probation Station.

They were there for three months. Ten more died—though only eight of these were victims of typhus. They were buried in a small cemetery on a point at Premaydena where some of their tombstones can still be seen, looking out across the waters of the bay to mountains which, on misty days, look remarkably like the Highlands of Scotland.

Richard Lord in his book, *Impression Bay: Convict Station to Civilian Quarantine Station*, gives many details of what happened during the three-month quarantine period—how the Rev John Seaman went at his own expense to tend the sick and teach English to the Gaelic speakers; how New Year's Eve was celebrated with a ball, vividly described in *The Hobart Town Courier* of January 6, 1858: how Mr John Loch, the Immigration Agent, inspected the catering arrangements, commended the meat and bread but thought the soup needed thickening with barley; how the people, according to Loch, showed every disposition to be satisfied …

'Satisfied' is an odd word to have used after all that these Highland families had endured, but the survivors of the typhus epidemic seem to have been a toughminded, resilient lot. According to *The Mercury* of November 6, 1857 they arrived at Impression Bay in good spirits, 'singing merrily as they were taken on shore'. On Boxing Day they held a fete at which one of their number climbed a greasy pole to win a leg of mutton 'with other delicacies', and, later on, a young female immigrant ran off with a convict constable. So, for some, life went on, though what became of the people from Harris and Coll, after their time of quarantine, I've yet to discover. One can only hope that eventually they settled down to their new country and—if they still had a taste for oatmeal—enjoyed their porridge in peace for years to come. It may be that some of their descendants—McDonalds, McKinnons, Morrisons— still live in the island state and will read this story over breakfast with *Leatherwood* propped up against a packet of their ancestors' traditional fare. Though, if there's a Scotsman on the packet one hopes he won't give anyone the idea that all his countrymen have always been as well-fed and carefree as himself.

Brazen hussy, golden-hearted treasure

Margaret has described herself, in poetics never published in this form, thus:

> *Plump cheeks split by shadows,*
> *a glint of spectacles, her horns and wisps of hair,*
> *brazen hussy, golden-hearted treasure,*
> *there is a great deal that I do not understand;*
> *stumping in muddy boots for a pot*
> *of fuchsia cuttings*
> *I can brood on reading the signs, on whether*
> *it's healthier to reflect or concentrate,*
> *angry at all that power to give or withhold*
> *held by a silly girl who broke with Nick,*
> *languished after a lanky history student,*
> *and married the one who could turn a compliment.*

Now, it should never again be published in this form, because it's not as good as in the various originals, which you'll all have recognised by now and seen that I have filched the lines from Margaret's poems here and there and strung them together. Not a classy trick, but it serves a distiller's purpose in the time allowed.

It disturbed me not to be able to weave in the marvellous couplet about poets, from 'Polishing the Step,' but I couldn't make it fit—with any felicity anyway—so I'm paying it a due nevertheless, unable to leave out those who:

> *Write verses damning brass and sluttish time*
> *and pin their faith on polishing a rhyme.*

Counterfeiting a poem of Margaret's, an enthralling aspect for me was to discover that I could not steal from 'Elegies'. It has far too much presence. It's too, well let's say it, sacred. I remember it as the first poetic work I'd read, of any subject, to make my heart gasp.

But we're not here to be serious for too long, we're here to love and we're here to party. So this is a more apt direction: in line with those games we play about where we were when man walked the moon, or when Whitlam was dismissed, or the Twin Towers fell, I'd be interested in a game which asks 'When was it for each of us that we fell in love with Margaret?' I'd lay money that the most common event for each of us was to do with an episode of her laughter. Margaret's laughter is an act of collaboration. Quite often it's about some astonishing tragedy.

It lays out some stunning absurdity, an absurdity perhaps in human suffering. It's subversive of disaster, a conspiracy of the human spirit. The frauds smirk, the dolts moan but, dear Margaret, the wise can't help but laugh.

John Bryson
Writer

The sisterhood

When I first began to travel about the Tasman Peninsula I was startled by the number of buildings described as 'old hospitals'. Things got to a stage where I'd say to my companion, 'What's that place? No, don't tell me—it's the old hospital.' And usually she'd say, 'Well, yes, it was.'

The most famous Peninsula hospital is, of course, the grim ruin at Port Arthur up on the hill above the penitentiary. This once imposing building, erected in 1842 to replace the original weatherboard hospital, could accommodate a hundred patients. There were four large wards, each presided over by a convict wardsman, and several small ones. I used to imagine these wards crowded with convicts recovering from one hundred lashes apiece but, in fact, by the time this brick and stone hospital had been completed, flogging was on the way out, soon to be replaced as punishment by solitary confinement in the new Model Prison. So the patients must have been men who had met with accidents while working in the saw pits or the blacksmith's shop, or people like the ill-starred Henry Savery, author of *Quintus Servinton* and Australia's first novelist, who was carried to the hospital after being laid low by a stroke.

About a month before he died Savery was visited at the hospital by David Burn, another literary pioneer whose drama, *The Bushrangers,* is said to be the first Australian play to be performed on a stage. Burn gazed upon the 'miserable felon' before him with 'sentiments of the deepest compassion mingled with horror and awe'. As well he might. Savery, well-born, personable and talented, had been given more than one chance of happiness and success, but a habit of using his fluent pen to write other people's names on bills of exchange had finally wrecked his life.

Henry Savery was only forty-eight years old at the time of his death. Other patients in the Port Arthur hospital may well have been older. It was by now almost forty years since the first contingent of convicts had landed in Van Diemen's Land. Provided their 'natural lives' had not been terminated, 'lifers' transported in the early years of the century were passing into old age, becoming infirm, going blind and losing their wits. Others who had served out their sentences were sometimes in a similar condition. This sad and motley band of 'invalids' and 'free paupers' had been separated by the British convict system from anyone who might have cared for them in their old age. They couldn't support themselves and they couldn't, or wouldn't, go away. From the 1840s onwards they began to weigh upon the system rather like the albatross which the Ancient Mariner was forced to wear round his neck as a penance for having shot it. Eventually, twenty years after the end of transportation, able-bodied convicts at Port Arthur would actually be outnumbered by those unfit to work—a host of aged dependants together with over a hundred younger 'lunatics'.

After the system of assigning convicts to free masters was abandoned in 1840, five probation stations were set up on the Tasman Peninsula: Slopen Island, Impression Bay (Premaydena), Cascades (Koonya), Wedge Bay (Nubeena) and Salt

Water River. In these stations, convicts were formed into gangs for various kinds of work, mostly timber-getting, milling or clearing the land for corn fields and vegetable gardens. And here, first at Wedge Bay, later at Salt Water River and Impression Bay, attempts were made to provide 'depots' for the reception of invalids, paupers or lunatics.

This meant building hospitals and one of these, a handsome brick building, is still quite definitely standing at Salt Water River. At Impression Bay the 'well ventilated and advantageously placed' hospital visited by Latrobe in 1846 has long since crumbled into rubble. Gone, too, are various other buildings that were pressed into service as hospitals at various times: the soldiers' barracks, converted to 'hospital accommodation' when Impression Bay became the colony's 'general invalid depot', and the 'large, airy' rooms that were used as wards for the fever patients carried ashore from the typhus ship *Persian* in 1857, after the invalids had been shifted back to Port Arthur. None of the few convict buildings still standing at Premaydena was ever, so far as I know, used as a hospital but, in view of the place's history, it's hardly surprising that, from time to time, someone tells you that the house where the station doctor lived or the storekeeper's cottage is one of the Peninsula's 'old hospitals'.

Along the road at Koonya there is another building with a much better claim to such a title. This is now a singularly beautiful private home belonging to the owners of Cascades Colonial Accommodation. For a long time I wondered why this hospital was erected when, so far as one can tell, no invalids or lunatics were ever sent to the probation station at Cascades. The answer seems to lie in the amount of timber-getting and milling that went on at the site. Felling and sawing the kind of trees that once covered the Koonya hills was a dangerous business even for experienced bushmen. For farm labourers from Devon or men who had grubbed a living from a Mayo potato patch the task of bringing down the tallest eucalypts in the world was more than doubly dangerous. Deaths were frequent and injuries plentiful enough to make the hospital an essential feature of the Cascades settlement.

Provided he escaped with his life, what could an injured timber-getter expect once he was carried up the hospital steps? If he had a crushed limb it would, almost certainly, have been amputated without any antiseptic agent or anaesthetic other than rum (if he was lucky). Thereafter all he could look forward to was a spell in a narrow bed, adequate food and, eventually, a place among the invalids. All this seems grim and meagre enough but it was, it appears, rather better than the treatment available in some other contemporary establishments.

In Britain all through the seventeenth and eighteenth centuries and the earlier decades of the nineteenth century—until, in fact, Florence Nightingale's reforms took effect—hospitals were generally places to be avoided. In 1831, if Captain Hamilton Wallace is to be believed, the situation was no better in the northern part of Van Diemen's Land. Captain Wallace complained that while he was a patient in the Launceston hospital he was kept awake by the shrieks of drunken women. The surgeon was a drunkard and the whole place nothing but a bawdy house. Elsewhere, in the Empire things were infinitely worse. When Miss Nightingale arrived in the military hospital at Scutari, for example, in 1854 she found the wounded from the battlefields of the Crimea lying in a filthy barrack-house, unventilated, swarming with vermin and bare of even the very simplest essentials—basins, soap, plates, cutlery. Even doctors were in short supply, though that may not have been quite the disadvantage one might imagine.

With some honourable exceptions, doctors were, for several centuries, even more lethal than hospitals. Things weren't too bad while they remained under the influence of the first-century Greek physician, Galen, but in the sixteenth century Western medicine began to turn away from Galen, who favoured herbal remedies, and fall under the sway of Paracelsus who favoured chemicals. Thereafter, as well as bleeding their patients, applying leeches with a free hand and recommending a dead chicken with its tail feathers plucked as a cure for plague sores, the medical profession set about making liberal use of substances such as copper sulphate, arsenic, sulphur and mercury.

As late as 1848 evidence given at a murder trial in Sussex revealed that a Dr Pocock had been treating a victim of arsenical poisoning with 'blue pills'. These contained such enormous quantities of mercury that it was difficult to decide who had actually finished off the dead man—the poisoner or the doctor. According to the diarist, G W T B Boyes, some Tasmanian practitioners were equally gung-ho in their procedures. He describes, for instance, how a Dr Bedford treated a case of erysipelas (an acute febrile disease characterised by deep-red inflammation of the skin). Whipping out a stick of caustic *(argenti nitras)* Dr Bedford passed it 'dexterously and artistically' about the patient's ear and face 'exactly as if stippling in the shadows of a portrait'.

This was in 1850. Although the news might not have reached Dr Bedford, the practice of medicine was about to be transformed. Antiseptics, vaccination, anaesthetics and the stethoscope were arriving in a rush, while in the Crimea, Miss Nightingale would soon begin teaching the Western world how to run its hospitals.

Although universally admired, Florence Nightingale is sometimes said to have been more of an administrator than a nurse and it is true that at Scutari she concerned herself with her patients' general welfare rather than with strictly medical matters. By one means or another she got the hospital clean and secured supplies of edible food, warm clothes and decent bedding. She also treated the soldiers as human beings. She set up reading rooms, started classes, helped them send part of their pay home to Britain and, above all, gave them hope. By these means she and her band of nurses reduced the mortality rate among the wounded at Scutari from 42 per cent to a little over two per cent.

To say that all this was not 'real nursing' seems to me to miss the point that the best and most successful nurses have always concerned themselves with their patients as whole people. Florence Nightingale didn't come out of a vacuum. She came from a wealthy family that had behind it a tradition in which women oversaw large households and, as part of their responsibilities, provided for the sick within a context of total care. Professional nurses from the past—figures like Dickens' Sarey Gamp—are far from appetising. But behind them, in the shadows, stand the ranks of home nurses who, though powerless to contend with, say, bubonic plague, undoubtedly saved a good many lives by keeping their patients warm, suitably fed, comfortably occupied and as hopeful as possible. One might say that these nurses stood at the cutting edge of holistic medicine. One might say the same thing of nurses practising today. Where a specialist may concentrate on ears, throats and noses—even noses alone—a nurse is always aware that a nose has a person attached to it.

That reflection brings us back to the Tasman Peninsula and the last of its old hospitals, one still intact and now used as a University Field Station, the other gone from its site at Salt Water River, leaving nothing but a rusting water tank and a patch of spring bulbs to show where it once stood. These two hospitals belonged to a time after the convict period and were set up to provide health care for the families who moved into the area after the Peninsula was opened to settlers.

The 'hospital' at Salt Water River was, in fact, a private house, the home of Sister Barnicoat and her husband, though, judging from the number of people who claim to have been born under her roof, part of the house must have served as a maternity ward at very frequent intervals. Sister Barnicoat's medical resources can't have been large by modern standards but, as she travelled about in the trap drawn by Jack, her light-coloured pony, she obviously made a huge difference to the families she visited. She has left behind an enviable reputation for dedication and skill and is remembered, according to Maurice Hallam, as 'doctor and friend to those people, especially the women, who lived on the Peninsula in the first quarter of this century'.

By 1930 the new bush hospital at Koonya had been built. It was here that Sister Clarice Mainwaring made her home. When she arrived in 1930 she was young, nervous and all too well aware that the nearest doctor was at Sorell, forty miles away. Her own equipment was, to say the least, meagre. The hospital had four beds but lacked electricity and was sometimes invaded by snakes. The medicine cabinet held nothing beyond aspirins, antiseptics and a few dressings. The nurse's car, a Waleys Whippet, was always breaking down despite the ministrations of a mechanic who kept his false teeth in his toolbox. But Sister Mainwaring did her best, trundling over dirt roads at night, trying to cope with gashed legs, amputated toes and difficult births. Sometimes, she says, she couldn't manage, but, even on these occasions, one suspects that she achieved more than she realised. People liked her. It helped to have her there.

Nowadays there are two doctors at Nubeena and a small modern hospital equipped in a way that neither the convict wardsman nor the bush nurse could possibly have imagined. All the same, the sense that one is being treated as a person rather than a case remains one of the most important remedies that the new hospital offers.

Sunburst of literary creativity

A great many years ago I sought out Margaret Scott for some advice. I wanted to know whether there was any point in continuing to write; whether the time had come to fix the focus of my life, singlemindedly, on climbing the slippery slope of academic promotion. Margaret's enthusiastically-tendered advice all those many years ago—and I am aware that it is not necessarily the advice she would give me today—was to soldier on. 'You are a writer,' she told me.

And so it was with a very great many of us. If it is the case, as I think it is, that Tasmania is currently the eye of an extraordinary sunburst of literary creativity, then this is due, in very large part, to the generous mentoring of Margaret Scott back in the 1970s and 1980s. She shaped and nurtured talents, often at the expense of her own preciously stored-up writing time. Literature and letters in Tasmania owe more to the selfless godmothering of Margaret Scott than any other individual.

When Margaret encouraged me to write she deflected me from the arid, disembodying abstraction of academic endeavour. She pointed me to the satisfactions of a grounded sensibility; of belonging, within the particularities of a single place. As a writer and erstwhile academic, and one who fetched up on our shores from the other side of the planet, these are tensions that are well-known to Margaret—indeed, such tensions are palpable within her writings, perhaps particularly so within her poetry. In all the brilliant works that have flowed from my island's poets over several decades now, there is no single piece that so enchants me than 'Encounter in Van Diemen's Land'. This is a brilliant, short and thoroughly accessible treatment of this very tension that I've been discussing. Standing for the 'old' Margaret, the displaced, thoroughly alienated migrant is old priest, who observes:

> Your children grow among the convicts' seed and
> no one of account was sent,
> only the scum of Ireland and the slums.

And then the 'new' Margaret, the Margaret at ease in her new island, lays the old ghosts of the past:

> The sea sighed and smiled.
> The wattle powdered the air.
> The garden shivered and grew and bred new life …

And:

> … the old man passed like a little stain
> and the changing, changeless mountain shone again.

Just marvellous. In her search for belonging Margaret has faced a journey much longer and more tortuous than my own. I, after all, was born here, and only had to discover, to animate, what had always lain within the marrow of my soul. Margaret is a wonderful Tasmanian writer, and she has nurtured the island, and been nurtured by it. How much the poorer would life here have been had she looked once at us, and taken the first transport out.

Pete Hay
Writer

Heydays & holidays

Until the prison at Port Arthur closed in 1877 and the Tasman Peninsula was opened to free settlers, the area beyond Eaglehawk Neck seemed an unlikely holiday destination. Yet, almost from its inception, the penal settlement attracted curious visitors. Some, like the Quaker travellers James Backhouse and George Washington Walker, had a special interest in penal reform, but plenty of other notable tourists with different backgrounds clearly felt that in Van Diemen's Land, Port Arthur stood at the top of the 'must see' list.

During his time as commandant of the prison, Charles O'Hara Booth did his best to put on a memorable show for visiting dignitaries. He arranged jaunts in his man-powered railway, which on the downhill run attained speeds 'tremendous … to lady-like nerves', and set up a display of makeshift rafts and coracles in which convicts had tried to escape. Even without these attractions Port Arthur remained a fascinating spectacle. It was, after all, Australia's largest prison, and in many ways its most progressive. Over the years all kinds of experiments could be observed: a semaphore system that could rely on over 11, 000 different signals; a steam-driven sawmill; the reformatory for juveniles at Point Puer; the farming of deer and angora goats; above all, the Model Prison, modelled on the state-of-the-art penitentiary at Pentonville.

Once the prison had closed, little of this remained, but the abandoned buildings still acted as a powerful magnet to sightseers. Some, like the poet James Hebblethwaite, came to engage in moral reflection, but most were more interested in thrills and chills. They set out from Hobart determined to have a good time and soon discovered that while a tour of the old prison gave a focal point to the excursion, the Peninsula had other pleasures to offer: sea-bathing, remarkable scenery, fishing, boating, bush picnics and rambles by the shore.

Day trips became popular. In 1889 a Boxing Day excursion to Port Arthur attracted a large crowd. They sailed from Hobart on the SS *Flora* accompanied by the garrison band, which according to a *Mercury* reporter, 'struck up a lively air', as they left the Argyle Street pier. On arrival at 'pleasant Port Arthur otherwise Carnarvon', the holidaymakers were entertained with footraces and chopping matches as well as a tour of 'this famous show place'. But with so much to see and do, a day was hardly enough, especially at a time when the journey from Hobart to the Peninsula took up so many hours. If, like the excursionists on the *Flora*, you sailed directly to Port Arthur and came straight home again, you could expect to be on the water for at least seven hours. If you went by boat to Nubeena on the Peninsula's west coast, or to one of the little ports on Norfolk Bay, the voyage was shorter but, after disembarking, you had to travel overland to the prison site in some kind of horse-drawn vehicle, so that the round trip could take you most of the day.

Adventurous spirits who set out to travel from Hobart to Port Arthur by road had first to cross the River Derwent by ferry, then take a train to Sorell. From there they journeyed on in a series of horse-drawn conveyances that, with luck, might get them to Port Arthur before dark. By about 1913 you could travel the whole distance in a hard-tyred Italia truck owned by the firm of Webster, Romech & Duncan. On the straight these trucks reached a speed of fifteen miles per hour, but they slowed to a quarter of that pace when climbing hills. Every four hours they had to stop so that the chains they were driven by could be greased. Barring accidents, an Italia could leave Hobart at 9:15 in the morning and make a detour beyond Eaglehawk Neck to take in the Blow Hole, Devils Kitchen, and Tasman Arch, and trundle into Port Arthur at about five o'clock in the evening. Naturally the passengers expected to spend the night on the Peninsula. And until the advent of more sophisticated coaches, family cars and better roads most visitors to Port Arthur had the same expectation.

Overnight accommodation took various forms. Some families boarded with friends, relatives, or a local householder glad of the chance to put an extra room to good use. Some, as time went on, rented pickers' huts or cottages. But the great majority were put up in the hotels and guesthouses that sprang up in almost every little settlement in the area. The former convict commissariat at Taranna became the Tasman Hotel and subsequently a guest house known as Taranna Lodge. At Wedge Bay (Nubeena), according to a *Mercury* report of 1889, 'a very nice and commodious house … furnished in a most comfortable and cosy style' offered refreshment and accommodation to an 'influx of visitors'. Lufra House opened as a health resort at Eaglehawk Neck in 1899, and in 1923 when Norman Dawn's cast and crew arrived at Port Arthur (otherwise Carnavon) to shoot the film *For the Term of His Natural Life,* they found three well-equipped establishments including the Arthur Hotel, which boasted hot and cold showers, a Butcher's fridge and a wireless set.

Despite the Depression and the Second World War, the years between 1920 and 1945 were, it seems, the golden age of the guesthouse and family hotel. These establishments flourished not just in Tasmania but in hundreds of other holiday resorts on the Australian mainland. In Britain they proliferated on windy headlands and filled entire streets in seaside towns. Their charges were usually very modest and, looking back, I can see that they were often run by people struggling desperately to make ends meet, but at the time, despite the discreetly patched sheets and faded curtains, they seemed to the children of my generation all that anyone could ask.

Thousands of people in their sixties, seventies and eighties remember childhood holidays in these places with almost frightening clarity. Memories of wedding days, births and deaths, wars and political upheavals may grow pale and dim, but Mrs Jones's potted palms and sepia photographs, her braised rabbit and gooseberry jam, the smell of her front parlour, the glimpse of glittering ocean from the bathroom window, the rasp of sand in gym shoes, and sandwiches cut for picnics—all these remain indelibly etched on the mind.

One reason for this may be that some sixty years ago, the fortnight's summer holiday stood out sharply from the rest of the year for families on both sides of the world. Very few of the people I knew in the late thirties or early forties owned motor cars, so that trips away from home were a rarity. All through the year we played hopscotch in the street, queued up at the local cinema on Saturday mornings, and went, as an occasional treat, to a circus or the zoo, but only on that one magical day in summer did we actually lock up the house, arrange for neighbours to water the tomatoes and feed the goldfish, and go right away from home to somewhere utterly different.

In the strange new world of the holidays, parents were transformed. One of the reasons for the popularity of the guesthouse was that in those days nearly all married women were housewives who worked away for fifty weeks of the year without any help from washing machines, microwave ovens, or food processors. Suddenly, released from their homes, mothers appeared in skirted bathing dresses and swam with stately strokes through gaggles of leaping children or turned into demon bowlers, pounding along the beach in hats and bloomers.

At mealtimes, relishing the experience of eating food cooked by somebody else, they indulged in the luxury of criticism. Dad, who had metamorphosed into an easy-going person with a sunburnt nose, always agreed that Mrs Jones's Windsor soup was watery ('not a patch on yours, dear'), but the disloyal children, ravished by the novelty of menu cards and butter pats, saw everything on their plates as wonderfully exotic.

Tasmanian friends who spent summer holidays at guesthouses like Mrs Barnett's Roseview at Port Arthur have uncannily similar memories. Mrs Barnett was probably way ahead of Mrs Jones in her cuisine, and the sense of 'getting away from it all' would have been stronger on the Peninsula than it was on the coast of Dorset or Devonshire, but the sense of entering a charmed world for two weeks, and the recollection of parents playing games, of daily ritual visits to the beach where you could scuffle away for hours with your bucket and spade in warm sand and bright water, of hearing the sound of the sea as you went to sleep—all this, it seems, we share.

After the Second World War things began to change. In England, as cars and freeways multiplied, people began to travel greater distances, even to venture across the Channel to Europe. Once Britain joined the EEC everyone wanted to see what they were getting into, so that people like my parents forgot about Mrs Jones and began to talk about coach tours and the Costa del Sol. In Australia, especially in Tasmania, things were rather different. Here, in the sixties, the weekend had become an institution. I was amazed to find on my first Saturday in Hobart that all the shops were shut and the place had turned into a ghost town. As roads improved and family cars became more common, half the population had discovered that they could get away to places like the Tasman Peninsula for two days in each week as well as for the traditional holiday in summer. Following that discovery, they found that regular weekend visits to their favourite beaches made the building of a 'weekender' worthwhile. Britain's decision to join the EEC had its effect here too. The orchardists of the Tasman Peninsula, faced with ruin and forced to pull up their trees, began selling off blocks of land for the building of shacks.

The *OED* gives several meanings for 'shack', including 'an idle, disreputable fellow' and a 'worthless horse'. The relevant one is 'a roughly built cabin or shanty of logs, mud etc'. And that is much what I expected to find when I was first offered the loan of a shack at Taranna. I drove down to the Peninsula with many misgivings and a boot-load of camping gear. The place turned out to be built—not so roughly—of oiled vertical boards and looked more like a cottage than a shanty. 'But,' we said to each other, 'there won't be much inside.' So we opened the door, expecting a few rough seats fashioned from logs, mud etc, and were struck dumb by the sight of carpets, curtains, comfortable chairs, an electric stove, a sink with taps … Opening off the central room there were well-equipped bedrooms and even a little bathroom with a shower.

I still remember the holiday that followed almost as clearly as I remember those summer fortnights with Mrs Jones. Afterwards we bought the shack at Taranna as our own weekender, becoming one of hundreds of families who, by this time, had holiday homes in nearly every part of the Peninsula. Most of these shacks were made, like ours, from vertical board or fibro sheeting. A lot were put up by their owners over six months of visits to 'the block', and furnished with bits and pieces dragged out from under the house or bought in junk shops in the days before every item over twenty years old became a collectable. Usually they were solid and comfortable without being grand—places were you could slop around in old jeans and not worry about getting sand in the rugs.

Children remember summers at the shack but not quite as vividly, I think, as my generation remembers its days with the likes of Mrs Jones. For one thing, you visit your shack more than once a year. There's no single shining fortnight standing out from months of greyness. And there's not quite the same sense of quitting home for the utterly different world that came with the guesthouse holiday. Instead, if you're lucky, you carry the best of home into another dimension. You do your own cooking, but it's fish caught that morning. The dog comes with you, but there's less fuss about him shedding hair over the carpet.

Looking around the Peninsula this summer I get the impression that the heyday of the shack, like that of the guesthouse earlier, is passing away. Tighter building controls mean that new dwellings are not vertical board cabins put up by families but professionally constructed houses that, often, are intended as future retirement homes. And as the rich get richer and the poor get poorer, the former head out to mainland cities and Pacific islands while the latter have trouble keeping one home going, let alone two.

Meanwhile Peninsula tourist operators offer facilities which combine some of the attractions of the guesthouse with those of the shack: serviced colonial accommodation for instance, or self-contained cabins and units. But, for the time being at least, most visitors come down the Arthur Highway in coaches that travel at six times the speed of the old *Italia* and, having looked around Port Arthur, return to the city before nightfall, like the excursionists of 1889 who sailed out from Hobart on the *Flora*.

Articulating the here and now

Margaret Scott taught in the English Department at the University of Tasmania from the mid-sixties until her retirement into full-time writing in 1989. I arrived at the university in 1968, just seventeen and eager to transcend my roots in the conservative/Liberal and introspective north of the state. When Margaret lectured us in English drama she began, involuntarily, aiding and abetting an incisive reassessment of my insular background. It was a wonderful upbringing I had, but there was a tinge of inferiority Tasmanians found hard to set aside in the face of strident voices from the other side.

She was British, Cambridge educated, confident, down-to-earth. She lacked that pretension I had known in achievers. Margaret Scott was one of the very few women role models on the horizon. The academic world was dominated by male lecturers and tutors, across all faculties. I spoke to her recently about the effect she had on me. She replied in that shock-sharp, self-deprecating way she has:

'What! In 1967 or 8 I could barely muster the strength to drag myself to lectures, I was always late and looking frightfully frumpy ... I was between two marriages, a ghastly time of late nights and domestic and maternal chores ...'

The picture she gave me shocked. Weren't those lectures rehearsed then? Perhaps they weren't even prepared! At eighteen or nineteen I was barely capable of empathy, let alone of understanding what my lecturer was going through before her hour-long discourses on seventeenth and eighteenth century British dramatists:

'The style of Congreve lifts him high above all his English rivals ... his dazzling scenes, a certain felicity of phrase ... limpid sentences, melodious and highly coloured... he stands on the threshold of the eighteenth century.'

She was then still in thrall of her English heritage and her memories which coloured her engaging delivery. Walking back to Jane Franklin Hall we girls would mimic just such a line and in a slow high-pitched, pained voice I would end it with 'Con-greve and Wych-erley ... ugh!' But I wouldn't have been a normal teenager if it had been otherwise. I marvelled that a woman could stand up the front and deliver with such a sustained focus on so obscure a topic. I was genuinely in awe of the literary background that infused her lectures.

But I was into marching against the war in Vietnam, protesting against the flooding of Lake Pedder, skiing all weekend and enjoying the freedom of the new gender equality with all the turbulence of youth thrown in as well. Nothing seemed remoter from the psychedelic sixties than that indulgent and pretentious Lady Wishfort in *The Way of the World* who would utter such tripe as 'Oh, I can never advance—I shall swoon if he sho'd expect advances. No, I hope Sir Rowland is better bred, than to put a Lady to the necessity of breaking her forms ...'

But it was precisely our reactions that Margaret had planned no doubt!! We were being exposed to a prodigal wit that is timeless and herein was the clue to our great teacher's philosophy: how is one to make the best of an imperfect world one cannot hope to alter? In her beloved dramatists—Marlowe included—Margaret could return to comedy in its purest sense at a time when she was flat out trying to reconcile all her own intractable realities. She was then still, I think, in agitated exile and ever so slowly coming to terms with the weird contrasts of her new home, its fierce history where her children must grow among 'convicts' seed' where 'graceless gum trees tittered in the sun' ('Encounter in Van Diemens Land' in *Visited*, Angus and Roberston,1983).

It is Margaret Scott's honesty that I have come to really appreciate through a belated study of her poetry. Her poems about everyday life—cooking and housework, gardening and child rearing—'Making Redcurrant Jelly' is a favourite of mine—are unpretentious and grounded. They reveal the secret of her ability to articulate the here and now. Thus the sheer range of her poetry, from the meditative, flow of conscience verse to rich historical insight, landscape and wildlife. And so she has become fiercely Tasmanian. This obsession in turn has informed her work for the community on the Tasman Peninsula, her marvellous witty pronouncements on the television program *Good News Week* and her frequent media comment on a range of social justice issues.

I have recently had the great honour of becoming reacquainted with my old lecturer; she has written a fine foreword to my anthology, *River of Verse* (Back River Press, 2004). Thankyou Margaret for the inspirational positivity and sense of fun that outshine your angst. You goad us all to rage, rage against the dying of the light.

Helen Gee
Editor, writer, activist

Life as a cultural icon

If *The Age* and the *Sydney Morning Herald* are to be believed, I have, late in life, changed from a 'a little known poet' to a 'cultural icon'. When I first read this announcement I was quite startled because I'd always thought that Australian cultural icons had to be extremely large—giant bananas or pineapples or sheep as big as the Sydney Opera House. I, on the other hand, am very small (no more than five feet or 152.5 centimetres even in my shoes) and the fame I've recently acquired is not exactly huge. Certainly I can't claim to be a megastar like (the former) Dame Edna. Still, Edna Everage and I do have one thing in common. Just at the point when we might have been expected to settle into placid grandmotherly obscurity, our lives have taken some very surprising turns.

As a result, I'm having a lot of fun. I'm not famous enough to find the attentions of either the media or the public at all intrusive. Nobody creeps up on my home to take photographs of my toes being sucked. (Not, of course, that anything other than a mosquito would care to batten on to my feet these days.) I don't get mobbed like a pop star or have my clothes ripped to shreds by manic fans. It's just that the world seems suddenly more welcoming. People I've never met beam at me and stop me at airports or in shops to say how much they enjoy the television program I've appeared on, *Good News Week*. Often, instead of having to scrabble around in my bag for some form of identification, I get waved on because the person on the other side of the ticket counter recognises my face. And I can impress the hell out of young friends and grandchildren by trespassing on the good nature of Paul McDermott, Mikey Robins and Julie McCrossin *(GNW* personalities) and getting them to provide batches of autographs to take home with me to Tasmania. Sometimes I even receive wonderful presents, including the best dessert wine and best big red I've ever tasted, sent down to the *GNW* offices by the generous owners of a vineyard near Orange.

Six years ago, if anyone had foreseen for me a future involving regular appearances on television, I'd have assumed they were deranged or drunk. After three years of retirement, I was enjoying life in the country, catching up with my family and friends, gardening and working intermittently on the odd poem and an assortment of novels. This, I imagined, was how things would be for the rest of my life. Occasionally I dreamed idly of fame, but I always thought that, if it came at all, it would come when I managed to produce the Great Novel or, possibly, the Great Collected Poems.

Then, in 1993, occurred an event that, though quite ordinary, was to have some curious consequences. At that time a Salamanca Writers Festival took place in Hobart every summer, and nearly always I, together with a number of other local writers, played some part in it. On this occasion I was asked to speak in a debate that promised to be pleasantly entertaining. The topic was 'There is no love sincerer than a love of food', and the guest speaker, leader of the affirmative team, was Alan Saunders, who presented his own food program on ABC Radio.

The evening went very smoothly. Both three-member teams performed creditably. Gwen Harwood, the poet, made a speech in rhymed verse. The audience of about 200 people laughed in the right places, and Ian Templeman from the National Library made an excellent moderator. I think the negative team—of which I was a member—won by a whisker, but it was a close-run thing, so that we all went home feeling cheerful and satisfied. And that might have been that, had not Alan Saunders decided to record the debate so he could use excerpts from the speeches as part of his radio show.

I knew nothing about this and so had no way of foreseeing what happened next. In those days, Ted Robinson was the ABC's head of comedy. The story I've been told is that one day Ted was driving along in his car, listening to Alan Saunders's food program, when he encountered the cigarette-stained voice of M Scott. Unfortunately, the script of that speech on the love of food has vanished and I can't remember much of what I said except that I lamented the demise of really lovable dishes like the pudding known as 'spotted dick', and claimed that modern nosh from nouvelle cuisine to the Big Mac just wasn't the stuff to inspire sincere love. Anyway, whatever Ted heard made him laugh so much that he had to pull off the road—or so he said to his colleagues when he got back to the ABC.

One of my favourite television shows in 1993 was *World Series Debating*. It was different from the traditional debating model—it was debate as entertainment. In each program there was a winning team and a losing one, but each session was self-contained. No team stayed intact to move on to another stage in an all-inclusive competition. There were hardly any rules except that the speakers were supposed to stop after eight minutes. Most went merrily on after the moderator had started ringing his bell, with H G Nelson, who once spoke for 16 minutes, holding the record for overrunning. The topics were chosen for their comic possibilities and so were the participants. The result was really six assorted comic monologues on a given theme rather than a contest in rational argument. The outcome was decided by acclaim, although the moderator, Campbell McComas, had to make up his mind which team had gained the louder applause.

At some point in the early months of 1994 I received a phone call from a woman who said her name was Gabrielle Ewington. She went on to explain that she was the producer of *World Series Debating*, then said, 'We heard about you doing a debate in Hobart and we wondered if you'd do one for us'.

'Now,' I thought, 'who is this smart-arsed little twit?'

Gabrielle began to talk rapidly and efficiently about the topic of the debate in which she wanted me to take part—'That beauty is better than brains'—the other participants, including Wendy Harmer, Tim Ferguson and Ita Buttrose; the team I was to join (affirmative); fees; hotels; planes. Slowly I realised that this was no joke. It was real. Gabrielle was a real producer, I was going to appear on a real TV show and I would have to come up with a real speech, arguing that beauty was better than brains. Not an easy assignment for someone who looks like me.

The State Theatre in Sydney is enormous. On Sunday 26 June, 1994, when I tottered onto the stage and saw well over two thousand people gazing at me from the stalls and crowded galleries, I thought I was going to faint with terror. I'd been given tickets for four friends but I couldn't see them anywhere. All the rest were strangers who had never heard of me and were probably wondering what on earth I was doing on the platform. I was, after all, female without being remotely glamorous, small, elderly, Tasmanian (which in Sydney usually means half-witted) and, worst of all, a poet. As I got up to speak, it seemed that most of the audience were cringing in their seats, expecting to be horribly embarrassed. Yet, in a way, that cheered me up. It struck me that, provided I could manage to stay vertical and utter a few words, everyone would applaud out of sheer relief. And I had my script, written in short sentences so that I wouldn't get breathless, clutched like a security blanket in my hand. It began like this:

'Ladies and Gentlemen, Beauty is better than brains. I hate to admit this. It goes against my ideology. I love the smell of a burning bra in the morning—nobody more. But unjust, deplorable as it may be, the beautiful have a better time than the brainy. Since I have a literary background I've been urged to stud my discourse with a few gems of deathless verse. Here's the first:

'Beautiful people are very tall like Elle Macpherson and Jerri Hall.

'Yes, beautiful girls have necks and long legs. When they do the kind of dancing where you don't lose your partner in the crowd, they enjoy eye-contact. But when I was a young person, brushing up on the fox-trot at Madame Adele's dancing class, my partner used to clap me to his stomach like a hot-water bottle on a nasty ache and roam off, staring into space. It was lonely down there, talking to a navel ... ' It wasn't all that funny, but the audience was so pleased that I made the distance that they went completely dotty. It was a great moment.

Afterwards there was a party in one of the theatre's upper rooms and after that the debaters and a large number of other people went on to a Chinese restaurant where we devoured a massive crab. By this time I was rather drunk on champagne and congratulations. I couldn't get over how nice everyone was to me. I'd expected the well-known professionals like Tim and Wendy to be rather distant, but they couldn't have been kinder or more helpful. The next *World Series Debate* was, for me at least, much less successful.

The topic was more difficult to handle— 'Australia is the arts end of the world'— and the element of surprise that had carried me forward in the first debate was now gone. This audience expected more and got rather less, so the whole thing was comparatively tame. After that there was a lull. Changes in the upper strata of the ABC's management led to the scrapping of *World Series Debating*. Then, in 1995, *Good News Week* began appearing on Friday evenings.

In the absence of offerings like *The Gillies Report* and *Rubbery Figures*, it was the only ABC show delivering a regular dose of political satire, though its targets were by no means always political. One of the program's most engaging features was that the three permanent members of the cast and many of their guests seemed willing to have a go at anything, so that you never knew what was coming next.

In case some readers haven't seen *GNW* I should explain that, basically, it's a parody of the ubiquitous game show with Paul McDermott as MC, Mikey Robins as leader of one team and Julie McCrossin as leader of the other. Every week each leader is joined by two guests, drawn from a mixed bag of comedians, actors, musicians, writers, politicians, sports stars and notable personalities of various kinds.

The show begins with a comic overview of the week's news and moves on to a series of games connected in some way with recent media reports. The teams might vie with each other in guessing names missing from a set of headlines or in picking the odd person out in a batch of famous faces. Points are awarded in a rather haphazard way and one team is usually pronounced the winner. Apart from Paul's opening survey and the links he uses throughout the show, the dialogue is unscripted. Everything the teams say and Paul's responses come off the cuff. Usually, the show is shot at the ABC's studios in Sydney in front of an audience of about 200, but sometimes it moves to another city—Melbourne, Perth, Brisbane—where the venue and audience are much larger. The whole program always runs for over an hour but is cut to half that length for broadcasting.

Although by 1996 I was quite a fan of *GNW* and relished its wacky energy and wit, I didn't see it as the kind of show that I might appear in. It must, I thought, be terrifying to have to try to be entertaining without a script. But when the phone call finally came, I agreed to take part, and I've never regretted it. Appearing as a member of Mikey's team can be difficult. For one thing, contrary to what many people believe, the teams get very little briefing. We're told what the games will be but we're not given the answers. So I always read the newspapers from cover to cover in the days before a show and hope that Mikey, who has an extraordinary breadth of knowledge and a close-to-photographic memory, will give me a few hints.

Sometimes, too, it's hard to get a word in edgeways, especially when someone like H G Nelson is on the team. But, despite all that, the whole experience of quitting my country retreat, flying to Sydney and feeling the rush of adrenalin as we take our places for the show is something I look forward to very much. It's fun to work with the *GNW* group, who are all quick, lively and extremely likeable; to meet people like Natasha Stott Despoja or Tim Farriss from INXS; to move for a day or two at a faster pace. I even enjoy being made up by an expert and staying at a hotel overlooking Sydney Harbour. And I enjoy getting home again, driving away from the airport and arriving finally in a place of dewy darkness, silence and the smell of freshly cut grass.

All this has changed my life, but the side effects of popping up regularly on TV have changed it even more. Apart from the pleasurable consequences of a very modest fame that I've already mentioned, being better known has brought a flood of invitations to write articles, to attend festivals and, above all, to give speeches of various kinds. At one stage, things got rather hectic with invitations of this kind arriving daily, so I put the whole business in the hands of my literary agent, so that my life now runs along quite smoothly but is still full of excitement and surprise. One day I might go off to Sydney to act as a commentator on the Tall Ships Race, flying out over the harbour in an orange boiler suit and a Red Baron helmet and enjoying my first trip in a helicopter. Another day I might go to Canberra to assist in launching a report on the quest for a new preamble to the Constitution. One thing is certain: life is never dull, and the future, though it sometimes looks alarming, is not, it seems, likely to be boring.

Backstage with Margaret

I remember being backstage at the ABC berating my poor producer Ted Robinson, 'you've given me some little old Tasmanian poet to work with, what are you doing to me mate!'

Ted then gave me one of his looks which usually meant shut up, calm down and trust me, I used to get that look quite a bit, and usually he was right.

An hour later we're sitting in the green room having a beer. Margaret had, of course, managed to single-handedly steal the show; she was sitting next to me breaking every ABC rule about smoking inside and also sipping on the scotch that would often mysteriously appear when she was on the show.

From then on her appearances became one of the highlights of the show, the outpouring of affection from a studio audience many decades younger than her seemed to bring her as much amusement as it did pleasure.

One of the things you wouldn't have seen was before the show when Paul, Julie and myself would introduce the guests, we always made sure to bring Margaret out last. Even the most secure performer would have dreaded having to follow the ovation her appearance on our stage would create, she was genuinely loved by the audience.

And why not, always funny, always wise and charming and able to say more with one askew glance than most folk can in a long monologue. Margaret, thanks for giving me some of my happiest moments on stage; to use an overused phrase, you're a bloody legend.

Mikey Robins
Comedian

Comic timing ...

Margaret Scott is quite simply the most intelligent and amusing woman I know. We first met on the set of the media quiz show *Good News Week* when it was on ABC television. It is rare for me to meet anyone smaller than myself. It is also unusual to meet a woman with a bigger personality than mine.

Margaret trumped me in both areas. We always performed *Good News Week* in front of a live audience. It was a highly competitive affair with all the comedians madly striving to get the camera to turn towards them, as they commented on the latest news.

Margaret was calm and quiet and yet the camera could not resist her. Her wit was as dry as the Australian desert. Her intelligence was unmistakable. Whenever she opened her mouth, the eyes and ears of everyone in the room were hers and hers alone.

I was awestruck and after the show I walked with her to her taxi at the entrance of the ABC. Margaret was very keen to get outside so she could light up a cigarette as quickly as possible.

Despite her obvious breathing difficulties at times, her passion for the fags was unmistakable. As I opened the door to her waiting taxi, I said 'Margaret, you are a comic genius and your timimg is impeccable'.

She looked at me drily and replied, 'That's not comic timing darling, that's emphysema'.

As I watched her taxi disappear into the darkness, I knew I'd been in the presence of a master.

It was a view shared by the *Good News Week* audience. Every time she came on the show, as Paul McDermott introduced her, the audience jumped to their feet and welcomed her with a standing ovation. And I was on my feet clapping too.

Julie McCrossin
Presenter of Life Matters on ABC Radio National.

The literary heritage

Tasmania has a literary history that dates from the earliest days of European settlement and can claim several Australian literary firsts. Yet as late as the 1840s, our writers were still in thrall to the British model and the Romantic styles of the late eighteenth and early nineteenth centuries. Gradually, in the process of coming to terms with our unique landscape, several Tasmanian writers were influential in pointing the way to a distinctively Australian voice that has bloomed and flourished in the twentieth century.

Like several other offshore islands—Ireland above all—Tasmania has produced over the years a crop of literary talent quite out of proportion to its limited population. And the development of Tasmania's poetry and prose, like many other aspects of life in the island state, represents a pared-down, intensely coloured version of the more complicated history that has unfolded on the Australian mainland—but with one major difference. Despite the damage done to Aboriginal culture, enough traditional songs and stories have survived in the mainland states to give us some idea of how words were used to create art in the years before whites arrived in Australia. But in Tasmania, the destruction of the indigenous tribes was so rapid that almost all knowledge of their poetry and myths has been swept away. As far as I know, nothing but the fragments of two songs remain.

The story of white Australian poetry begins with the convict ballad, which might be either a feisty piece damning 'gags and cats and chains and traps and cruel tyranny' or a sad lament filled with regret and longing for the old home far across the sea. True to form, Tasmania produced one of the most fiercely rebellious of all convict ballads, 'The Seizure of the Cyprus Brig', as well as one of the most plaintive, 'Van Diemen's Land', which tells of the miseries endured by Tom Brown, Jack Williams and 'poor Joe', all transported from their native land for poaching. The tale of the group of convicts who managed to overcome their guards and gain control of the *Cyprus*, while on their way from Hobart to Macquarie Harbour, has been attributed to Frank McNamara or 'Frank the Poet', who was transported to Van Diemen's Land in the 1820s. Individuals like 'Frank' or groups of anonymous convicts were responsible, no doubt, for other similar ballads, but the origin of laments like 'Van Diemen's Land' is more questionable. There is a theory that some of the more heartrending ballads were composed by government hacks as awful warnings to would-be criminals and started life in London as broadsheets sold in the streets.

Convict ballads are, of course, based on British models; so, too, was the verse written in the early years of the nineteenth century by members of Australia's free population. Some of these poets looked back to the style of the previous century. Using rhyming couplets and lofty diction, they focused on society rather than the individual and usually saw the beauties of nature as no more than a background for human achievement. One of the best examples is 'Tasmania, A poem' by 'P-', which appeared in the *Hobart Town Magazine* in 1834. Having pointed out 'stern

Mount Wellington' and 'glorious' Mount Nelson, 'P-' turns on the young township of Hobart.

> *Girt by such mountains, towering to the skies—Urged by such names, thou must! thou shalt arise!*

Other poets of the time were less enthusiastic about their new surroundings. Writing in the more flexible style of Romantic poets such as Wordsworth and Keats, they produced verses which, unlike the works of 'P-', were much concerned with personal feeling and the natural world. Often the feelings expressed were grief and homesickness, and the natural world was the remembered countryside of England, seen as infinitely more lovable than anything the Australian colonies could offer.

> *Ye may tell me of flowers of crimson hue And glorious tints of gold and blue …*

wrote Caroline Leakey during her extended visit to Tasmania in the 1840s,

> *But oh! for the meadows of England's green, Set thick with the golden kingcups' sheen.*

One is left wondering whether poets like Caroline Leakey ever really took a proper look at any part of their new surroundings. Yet even as she was composing her 'Attempts to Sing in a Strange Land', a great change was coming about in Australian poetry. For the first time, poets were beginning to pay close attention to the colonial landscape and to celebrate it in their writing. As usual, this general shift is exemplified particularly clearly in the work of a Tasmanian writer—in this instance, the remarkably gifted Louisa Anne Meredith.

Louisa Anne Meredith had already established a reputation as a poet and painter of flowers before she left England with her husband in 1839, and when she settled in Tasmania she began examining the landscape around her with an eye accustomed to recording precise botanical details. As she explored, she experienced a wonder and delight which she managed to express in her writing:

> *… caladenias quaint, with hoods and fringes rare, Couched by old mossy trees midst delicate maiden-hair, Acres of peaty swamp glowed purple with the shimmer Of gay rush-lilies; and in dells where the forest shades fell dimmer—*
> *In deep, green, silent glens—silent, except the fall Of tinkling streams that made a monotone most musical—*
> *The feathery fern trees dwelt, with palmy crests outspread, Close interweaved and overlapp'd in canopies overhead…*

As well as being a notable poet, Meredith was one of the many prose writers who worked in Tasmania during the earlier part of the nineteenth century. Between them, they produced almost every kind of prose composition imaginable: letters, journals, essays, histories, travelogues, plays, novels and a crop of newspapers which sprang up like mushrooms and sometimes disappeared as quickly. Some of this material has never been edited or published and much of it is less well-known than it deserves to be. A case in point is John Mitchel's *Jail Journal*—or at least the journal's Tasmanian sections, which have been edited by Peter O'Shaughnessy and published separately as *The Gardens of Hell: John Mitchel in Van Diemen's Land 1850-1853*.

Mitchel, together with six other members of the Young Irelanders' group, was convicted of offences relating to his rejection of British rule in Ireland and transported to Tasmania, where he was placed under house arrest. While living in a cottage at Bothwell on the fringe of the Central Highlands, he wrote:

In vain I try to torment myself into a state if chronic savage indignation—it will not do here. In vain I reflect that ... I am, after all, in a real cell, hulk or dungeon... that these ancient mountains with the cloud-shadows flying over their far-stretching woodlands are but ... prison walls—that the bright birds waving their rainbow wings, here before me, are but 'ticket-of-leave' birds, and enjoy only 'comparative liberty'.

Mitchel escaped to New York in 1853, but before he left he built up a personal record which has been hailed in Ireland as a masterpiece and named by the Tasmanian novelist C J Koch as his favourite book. Koch once remarked that his friend, the poet Vivian Smith, had said that 'a country and its landscapes perhaps don't fully exist until they have been written about—until poets and novelists create them'. John Mitchel was preoccupied by this idea, dwelling on it as he explored the lakes and mountains around Bothwell:

Why should not Lake Sorell also be famous? Where gleams and ripple, purer, glassier water, mirroring a brighter sky? Where does the wild duck find securer nest than under the tea-tree fringe, O lake of the south? ... Some sweet singer shall berhyme thee yet, beautiful lake of the woods ... Haunted art thou now by native devils only... but the spirits of the great and good who are yet to be bred in this southern hemisphere shall hover over thy wooded promontories in the years to come ...

Although Lake Sorell has never achieved the degree of fame Mitchel envisaged, unknown to him, Tasmanian writers, often using Tasmanian settings in their work, had already begun to lead the Australian literary field. The island's early prose writers in particular chalked up a remarkable number of firsts, including the first novel and the first collection of essays to be written and published in Australia. These books, *Quintus Servinton* and *The Hermit in Van Diemen's Land*, were both the work of one man: the volatile Henry Savery, who began life as the son of a wealthy English banker and ended it, dying probably by his own hand, as a convicted felon. Unhappily, despite several chances to make a fresh start, Savery could not resist using his ready pen to sign other people's names on bills of exchange—a practice which led first to his transportation to Van Diemen's Land and later to incarceration at Port Arthur. Here, as he lay in the prison hospital, Savery was visited shortly before his death by David Burn, who left a moving account of the visit:

I could not contemplate the miserable felon before me without sentiments of the deepest compassion mingled with horror and awe.

It was a significant moment for Australian literature, since Burn was also the author of two works which can be claimed as firsts, not simply for Tasmania but for the Australian colonies. One of these was *The Bushrangers*, the first Australian drama to be performed on a stage, while the second, *Plays and Fugitive Pieces*, was the first dramatic work to be printed and published in Australia. This production, bound in two volumes 'enriched with Californian gold', was one of the exhibits from Tasmania displayed in London at the Great Exhibition of 1851.

As Burn sat contemplating 'the once celebrated Bristol sugar-baker—a man upon whose birth Fortune smiled', reduced now to disgrace and despair, one imagines a great quiet, as though these two founding fathers of Australian and Tasmanian literature were at the eye of a storm. Around them, the new literary world of the colonies seethed with disputes, which at one time or another affected the careers of both Savery and Burn. Lieutenant-Governor Arthur, in particular, bitterly resented criticism and often pursued newspaper editors or the authors of objectionable books with libel suits or charges of contempt of court. Burn, recognising that *The Bushrangers* dealt with a touchy subject— the Brady gang's ability to make a fool of Arthur—arranged for his play to be staged in Scotland rather than Van Diemen's Land. But Savery—typically—blundered into trouble over the publication of his 'Hermit' essays in the *Colonial Times,* and later lost his ticket-of-leave when he was falsely accused of writing an anti-Arthur piece for *The Tasmanian.*

As the years went by, the conflicts into which Australian writers were drawn became generally more literary and less political. There was, for instance, long-drawn-out resistance to the huge changes brought about by the advance of modernism in other parts of the world, and another related battle over how specifically Australian the writings of this country ought to be. A group known as the 'Jindyworobaks' insisted that Australian poets should concentrate on depicting the Australian way of life, along with landscapes and wildlife which are found nowhere else, while poets such as A D Hope rejected attempts to restrict Australian poetry to a celebration of 'the stockwhip and the spur'. In Tasmania, the work of two very different women poets who lived and wrote in the state between World War I and World War II exemplifies some part of these extended literary battles. The first, Helen Power, used traditional rhythms and rhyme schemes in her work and, while she might sometimes mention, say, a Tasmanian magpie, drew many of her images from classical mythology and European literature. In the 1930s, she found that magazine editors had begun to reject her verses as 'not sufficiently Australian in tone', so she ceased to write until, in old age, she suddenly produced a number of new pieces in fashionable free verse.

Norma Davis, on the other hand, engaged in more technical experiments than Power and yet, at the same time, concentrated in her first, more notable book on the scenes and creatures she discovered in the countryside near her home in the Tasmanian Midlands.

After World War II, there was a great upsurge of poetic activity in Australia as a new generation of poets—powerful, but mistrustful of modernism—came to fame. Then, in the 1960s, another wave of poets rose up, challenged the old guard and opened the door to a torrent of new ideas from across the world. Today, there are hundreds of poets working in Australia, free very largely of the nagging question of whether their poetry is sufficiently Australian in tone and open to a huge range of different influences. In Tasmania, there has been a similar poetic renaissance. In the early 1950s, two young writers, Vivian Smith and C J Koch, appeared at the same moment over the literary horizon. When their work was included in *The Penguin Book of Australian Verse,* published in 1958, the editors remarked: 'It may be taken as a sign of hope, at least, that after a century and a half of silence, broken only by the minor lyrics of James Hebblethwaite and Norma Davis, Tasmania should produce two young poets of such promise and almost simultaneously.' This comment is, of course, utterly mistaken in reducing Tasmania's earlier poets to no more than two, although it has to be admitted that in the years immediately before the emergence of Koch and Smith, the stream of Tasmanian poetry was running pretty low. The Penguin editors were, however, absolutely correct in seeing the rise of the two young poets as a sign of hope. Both have gone on to become important Australian writers, although C J Koch is now better known as a novelist than as a poet. Meanwhile, in the island of their birth, poetry has blossomed as never before.

Soon after the appearance of the Penguin anthology, another poet arrived in Tasmania: James McAuley, who was already well known. And another, Gwen Harwood, who started publishing poetry before 1958, would go on later to win every major literary award in Australia and become a national treasure. Over the past two or three decades more and more poets have settled in Tasmania, more local talent has been fostered and Hobart has been hailed as the poetry capital of Australia.

Tasmania's prose writing, especially its fiction, has also prospered in recent years although there has been no spectacular revival of the kind seen in poetry. But then, the stream of novels and short stories which can be claimed as Tasmanian has never run as low as the level of the island's poetry in the 1940s. In this, as usual, Tasmania's literary scene represents in miniature what has happened in mainland Australia, where the flow of fiction has run on unabated from the 1830s to the present day.

And at least one change that has taken place in the general nature of Australian fiction during those years can be seen particularly clearly in the writing of the island state. This is a shift from fiction that uses Australian material as exotic flavouring designed to intrigue an overseas audience to something very different—to writing which is much less self-consciously Australian and much more concerned to explore, for a home-grown readership, the society from which it has sprung. At the start stand stories of bushrangers and marauding blacks, which, like Charles Rowcroft's *Tales of the Colonies, or The Adventures of an Emigrant* (1843), were popular in England.

More than 150 years later comes Richard Flanagan's *The Sound of One Hand Clapping*, which is also concerned with the adventures of an emigrant but which sets out not to entertain a foreign readership but to hold up a mirror to a local one. In the years between came romances like Marie Bjelke-Petersen's *The Captive Singer* and *Jewelled Nights*, which were set largely in Tasmania but published, with remarkable success, in London. Or, later, novels of social criticism such as Hal Porter's *The Tilted Cross*. Tasmania has, of course, featured repeatedly as a setting in a host of novels and stories by mainland authors ranging from the most famous of all convict novels, Marcus Clarke's *For the Term of His Natural Life*, to Martin Boyd's chronicles of the Langton family. Usually the island has been presented as a place quite alien to mainland Australia, somewhere that is either a prison or a scene from childhood, somewhere to be left behind when one becomes free or reaches maturity. Yet now it seems that things are changing again. Just as, say, Tim Winton's *Cloudstreet*—uncompromisingly Australian and addressed apparently to a local audience—has won popularity with readers overseas, so Richard Flanagan's quintessentially Tasmanian novels are achieving international success. And, paradoxically, *The Sound of One Hand Clapping* in particular, has been accepted throughout mainland Australia as much more than a tale belonging to the little island on the other side of Bass Strait. It has been received as relevant to the whole of a society in which all whites are migrants or the descendants of migrants. This, perhaps, constitutes a sign of hope for both Tasmanian and mainland writing even more significant than the rebirth of the island's poetry.

A day in the life of Margaret Scott

For several years I have typed Margaret's manuscripts, letters, speeches, etc and during some fairly frenetic periods, I would spend three to five days a week with her. She was not good at deadlines! In fact, I have often heard her say, 'Trish, I have this problem … !' I knew what that would mean. Either she had totally forgotten an appointment at which she was to be the key speaker and hadn't even thought about her subject, or the deadline for the book had come and gone and we were only halfway there. I have to say there would be mutterings under my breath during those times, especially when I would find several logic puzzle books lying around amongst the writings. I knew precisely why she didn't finish on time.

Although there were some tense moments, most of the time it was fun and I felt absolutely privileged to be working with this remarkable woman. I have very fond memories sitting with her at her huge table in the kitchen of her beautiful Federation home, Tara, discussing the plot(s) and characters of the latest book. Sometimes I felt quite daunted by the mind and the ideas that would come from that mind, other times I would get up the courage to argue a point with her. Which, I must say, she would usually accept graciously. Often we would share our lunch with Denis, an old friend of Margaret's who would come down from Hobart one day a week to help in the garden. These were great moments when we would discuss the world and its problems. Quite often she would sound us out with several jokes she had found which she was going to use on *Good News Week* or in one of her keynote speeches. Margaret loves jokes and takes great delight in telling them. She's like a small child, grinning from ear to ear as she works her way to the punch line. Some days there would be another poet, author or academic who would pop in with a bottle of wine and cheese to share. I will always hold those days dear. I will never forget that house or the garden around which I ambled on many a day, while she would sit in her living room writing furiously so I could get on with the typing!

My husband, James, has also worked closely with Margaret. Together they have established the Tasman Institute for Conservation and Convict Studies. It has always been Margaret's dream to have a postgraduate establishment here on the Tasman Peninsula and, gradually, with a lot of hard work and a great deal of time, TICCS is bringing together academics and professional people towards that aim. I have also been very much involved in setting up this organisation, including many dinner parties at which great discussions, interspersed with much hilarity, would take place. Once again, there have been some tense moments—but on the whole there has been much more fun. Trying to organise the 'emphysemic poet'—as James refers to her—into the car with wheelchair, oxygen tank and a spare one just in case, is an amazing exercise. This we have done often, with me sitting in the back, listening to her relate one of her many stories all the way to Hobart, or, giggling to myself as she and James would argue some point of great importance, but which was always interspersed with much wit from both of them.

Trisha Parker
Transcriber